You Can Become Successful

(Discover the Secrets of High Achieving People)

By Victor Dedaj

2017

Front and Back Cover Photos by Christopher O'Hare

Intro

You can become successful. There have been millions and millions of people who have done it before you. Many of them are not any smarter or more talented than you are. If they can do it, then you can do it.

You will have ups and downs, and at times you may feel like quitting, but if you persevere to the end, the payoff will be awesome.

Some of the people you'll read about in this book had struggles similar to yours and mine, and some even tougher. These people had certain habits that most unsuccessful people do not have, which allowed them to achieve great things. I hope you will be able to attain amazing results yourself after reading this book.

A Little About Myself

My name is Victor Dedaj. I was born and raised in the Bronx, New York. My parents were immigrants from the Balkans. They came to the United State for a better life. They were both very hard working. They were supers in a small building for a while, then got a building of their own where tenants paid us rent.

I learned when I was young that you could make residual income in addition to getting paid for working at a job. I never forgot that there were various ways to make money, in addition to working a job.

Eventually, we moved from that building to a house in a nicer neighborhood. We had to sell the building because none of the supers we hired panned out, and since the neighborhood had gotten dangerous, my dad did not want us going to that neighborhood to collect the rent because he feared us getting hurt. Our safety was the most important thing to him.

Still, I always remembered that you could make money besides by working for someone else at a regular job.

When I finished college, I went to work in the corporate world. I worked in operations for a number of years and then worked as a performance analyst for many years after that. As time went on, I really was not happy doing what I was doing. I slowly came to the realization that I was not meant to work in the corporate world, and that was why I was not happy there. I felt like I was in a rut.

When you are not passionate about what you do, you won't be happy doing it and you won't be as creative or as productive as when you work on something that you thoroughly enjoy doing. You will also be miserable and won't succeed in the long run.

I am not saying there is something terribly wrong with working in the corporate world. I have many friends working in the corporate world who love it. I also made a lot of wonderful friends there who I am still friends with after all these years. It just was not for me. I realized after a while I was not very happy or passionate about what I was doing. When you are not passionate, you are not excited to get up in the morning and do what you do, because you don't love what you do.

After working two decades in the corporate world, I was let go from my job in 2013. I actually was relieved. I did not enjoy what I was doing.

I had hated commuting to Connecticut for work. Since I did not have a car, I had to walk to the bus stop and get a bus to the railroad that went to Stamford. From the Stamford train station, I had a 15- minute walk. Altogether it took me an hour and a half to get to work. And of course, it took me an hour and a half to go home. That was 3 hours just for commuting. That wears on you after a while.

What was nice was the Friday I got let go was also my birthday weekend, and there were a number of events going on where I celebrated my birthday. I had an amazing time celebrating with my friends for 3 consecutive days. I felt so free and happy.

It was nice having a little break after working straight for almost two decades. I realized that the corporate world was not for me. Even if I got another job, I would probably get a big pay cut with how horrible the job market was. Plus, I was tired of having other people telling me what to do, and of having limited options.

I wanted to work for myself and work from home, and not have a commute. When I used to live in Midtown Manhattan and worked in Midtown Manhattan, I would walk to work. I wanted to have a very short commute where I was not dependent on public transportation.

Now that I work from home, I commute from my bedroom to my workroom, which is about 1 minute. It's nice having that extra 3 hours to myself. Commuting really takes a lot out of a person. I live in New York City, and we commute the most out of any people in America. We get up early and work late.

It's not a great way to live. It seems a lot of people live to work instead of work to live.

I remember the group Loverboy came out with a song in the 1980's called "Working for the Weekend." The sad truth is that most people live solely for the weekend. They try to get by through the week, just so they can enjoy a couple of days off. I was that way for many years.

I would also often get the Sunday night stress anxiety that many people get, dreading to go to work Monday mornings. I would get stressed out many Sunday evenings. It also did not help that I often had meetings on Mondays. That is not a healthy way to live. I know from my experience in the corporate world that many people feel the same way.

Research shows that most heart attacks occur Monday mornings. Some people say that most people would rather die than go to work. It turns out that stress is a big factor in those Monday morning heart attacks. Long-term stress is a silent killer, and it affects many working people today. I used to feel that stress. Thankfully I don't feel that stress anymore.

Nowadays pretty much any day is a weekend day for me. I remember looking forward to three day weekends to have that extra day off. Now those long weekends don't really matter much to me. Every day is the same to me. I can take off work whenever I feel like it. I can go on vacation whenever I want and don't have to get permission from a boss. I don't have to wait until Friday to enjoy my life.

I love what I do, which is being an entrepreneur. I am very passionate about being an entrepreneur and helping people succeed. I look forward to each day and am excited because of the chance to help people and make a huge difference in their lives.

I want to help people believe in their dreams and help them believe that they can do great things with their lives. When you encourage people and help them believe in themselves, you never know what kind of effect it can have on their lives.

I will say that there were some great benefits in the corporate world. I did make a lot of nice friends over the years, and I had some great bosses in most of my jobs. The problem was the big bosses had the final say and not my immediate bosses. That took away some of the benefits from the job.

Things happened that I had no control over. Even though I had a number of good bosses over the years, they would not always last. What sometimes happened was that the company would bring a new director in, and they would have no loyalty to the team, so they would often force out my boss out and bring in their own person. The new boss usually was nowhere near as good, and that sometimes made my life difficult. I realized that things could always change in the corporate world and some things I had absolutely no control over.

I realize that many employees feel the same way. They feel powerless to change their situation. With the job market being difficult for many years, it's not easy for them to switch to another job. Many jobs that are out there actually pay lower than what people are used to making.

One of the toughest things for me to overcome when I decided to become an entrepreneur, was the employee attitude that I had developed working almost two decades in the corporate world. I basically did whatever I was told to do, and did not think too much for myself, and was not very entrepreneurial. Part of it was that the corporate culture did not allow for it. You have to tow the company line and fit into the culture of the company.

So when I decided to work for myself, it was very hard not having superiors tell me what to do, and believing I could succeed on my own and be my own boss, because I had always had bosses. There was a struggle in my mind. Part of me enjoyed the freedom, and part of me was not used to not being told what to do.

I came to realize that mindset is very important. It's not enough to have the skills. If you don't have the mindset that you can succeed, then no matter how talented you are, you won't succeed. You have to develop the mindset that you can succeed.

Have you ever seen a sports athlete who you know had the talent to be a hall of fame player, yet for some reason never became a consistent all-star? Why is that the case? Many times it is because the person has a poor mindset. He does not believe in himself enough and does not have the confidence to believe that he can be a champion. Until he changes his mindset, nothing will change for that athlete.

That is also why you will see a pitcher, who is a talented pitcher but has a losing record for a losing team in baseball, does not become a winner when he gets traded to a winning team. All those years of losing have taught the pitcher to lose in his mind. Since he has developed a losing mindset, he rarely becomes a 20 game winner when he gets traded to the good team. He often is just a .500 pitcher with his new team.

A lot of baseball teams don't understand that and will continue trading for these talented pitchers on losing teams, and those pitchers don't do much with their new team.

My mindset definitely held me back in the past. For a long time, I was interested in having my own business. The problem was that working in the corporate world for many years, I developed an employee mentality. I did not truly believe that I could succeed on my own, even though I did want to have my own business. I believed that the only way to succeed was to work for someone and have a boss tell me what to do. That is why I hesitated trying to start my own business.

Sadly, many new entrepreneurs don't want to learn about mindset. They think it's not important. They just want to learn the technical aspects of becoming successful. While that is definitely important, if you don't develop the proper mindset, even if money comes your way, you will find a way to lose it or get rid of it. That is a major reason why most lottery winners are broke within 5 years. Maybe they feel guilty or undeserving of the money, or maybe they learned as kids that rich people are immoral and greedy, and subconsciously don't want the money. As a result, they don't have the proper mindset for having all that money, so they find a way to spend it.

I decided to surround myself with people who are successful and who have positive mindsets. If you want to become better at something, you need surround yourself with people who are better at it than you are. If you surround yourself with people who are worse at it than you are, then you won't get any better.

Mark Victor Hansen recounts in the book "The Aladdin Factor", how he and Tony Robbins both spoke at an event in New York City for the New York Chiropractic Society. Hansen asked Robbins how Tony was able to make 50 million each year, while Hansen and his partner Jack Canfield only made a million a year, even though they were just as smart as Robbins.

Robbins asked him "How much money do each of the people in your mastermind alliance make?"

Mark Victor Hansen said they made about a million or so each year.

Tony Robbins said that was the problem. Tony continued, "Everyone in my group makes 100 million a year. You need to surround yourself with people that are already manifesting at the level you want to reach. They will stretch you into a bigger game."

What a lesson to learn. Hansen and his partner Jack Canfield have gone on to attain much bigger success. That is why I am always looking to surround myself with more successful people because I want to be around people who are already manifesting what I want, and who will help me stretch.

You don't have to make 50 million like Tony Robbins did. Perhaps you are making $50,000 or $100,00 a year, and want to increase that to $500,000 or $1,000,000. What you need to do is to surround yourself with people that are manifesting that level and who will make you stretch to do more.

I also devour as many books and videos by successful people, as well as biographies of successful people. Contrary to popular opinion, many successful people were not born rich. They were born middle class or poor. Many of them had tremendous obstacles they had to overcome.

There is so much negativity out there, and since I had a mindset that was negative before, I needed to avoid negativity and become exposed to as much as positive influences as possible.

Reading is helpful as it gives you lots of knowledge. Successful people realize that learning does not stop when you finish high school or college, but continues for the rest of your life. As long as you see yourself as a student and are willing to continue learning, you will be successful.

You don't have to read a lot each day to become very knowledgeable. You can read 10 pages of a good book each day and by the end of one year, you will have read 3,650 pages. That is a lot of learning in one year. The key is you need to be consistent.

I have read a lot of books on marketing and personal development. I remember Jim Rohn saying that if you work hard on your job, you can make a living. And if you work hard on yourself, you can make a fortune. He was so right. Most marketers don't do this.

They say that leaders are readers and that learners are earners. I read that the average CEO reads 5 books a month, which is 60 books a year. The average American reads 1 book a year. That is one reason CEO's make a lot more money than the average employee. CEO's read because they know they may learn one or two things from a book that can change their lives.

Unfortunately, many people think learning stops after school. Nothing can be further from the truth, especially in this day and age. It's not like the old days where a person worked for IBM and stayed there for their entire career. The days of working at one company for your entire career are gone. People will change their careers several times during their lives.

Technology is rapidly changing, and you have to keep on top of all the changes, otherwise you will get left behind. They say that if you are not growing, then you are dying. One way to look at things is to realize that because of technology, most of the jobs that will be around 20 years from now have not even been invented yet.

When I listen to a very successful entrepreneur quote a book they like, I often go and buy the book, and most of the time the books are great and I learn some useful things that can help me in my businesses.

You have to constantly keep learning. I do my reading in the morning to make sure I get some learning done before I do my regular work. I also like to get my subconscious mind filled with positive and powerful stuff in the morning.

I also meditate for 15 to 20 minutes a day. Just as we have to detox our bodies from time to time of junk, we also have to detox our minds. When your mind is cluttered with so much stuff, it is difficult to get stuff done and to be successful. When you meditate and focus on one thing or one word, you will be a lot more effective as you clear out your mind.

I also do some visualization every day. I visualize the kind of life I desire. Many people are not aware that subconscious mind cannot differentiate between real and imagined events. The more you focus on the kind of life you want, the more your subconscious will work to make it a reality.

It is amazing that once you start achieving some success, it seems to become an avalanche. All of a sudden, people start noticing you, and want to work with you.

When you develop yourself and become a person of value who helps people, people will be drawn to you, and you will make a lot more money.

One problem many internet marketers have, and a problem I also had, was falling prey to instant gratification. Internet marketers want instant results without putting in the effort and developing themselves. One reason is that we are in a digital age where we can get everything instantly and find out information instantly. As a result, when we start an online business, we expect to make money instantly.

When we were an agrarian society, we understood that a farmer had to plant in the spring, cultivate for 5 or 6 months, and then harvest in the fall. They knew they had to cultivate for a few months before they could harvest the crops.

Nowadays it seems many newbie marketers want to plant and immediately harvest. They don't want to cultivate. It just does not work that way. There are no overnight successes. All of the people who seem to be overnight successes were people who put in the effort for years, and because they didn't quit and give up, they achieved success.

Another problem I dealt with was something called shiny object syndrome. I would join a business opportunity, and then another one would pop up, and I would join that one. Then another one would appear, and I would join that as well. I would be in 3 or 4 companies and would be overwhelmed trying to promote all of them and would get paralyzed and not do anything in any of the companies.

It was difficult to see other people succeeding while I could not seem to get to the next level. I helped a lot of people out, but a lot of them would not join me. It seemed that they would go to me for free advice, and then join someone else. I felt like the guy who girls would tell all their secrets to, but not the guy they would date. Still, I persevered.

Things started improving in my businesses, and I started to experience success. I was starting to develop momentum in my businesses.

I then learned that as an entrepreneur, you will experience obstacles on your road to success.

I started getting sick in the spring of 2015. It turned out to be a very difficult time. I had pains in my back. I thought it might be a urinary tract infection.

I went to see several doctors, and also went to the emergency room several times. Everyone told me I was fine. The only thing that stood out was that my blood pressure was high.

Even though they told me I was fine, I knew I wasn't. Something was not right. I had bad headaches, felt dizziness, and had very low energy. I could not even go out and walk more than a few blocks. I could not even read a book.

I had terrible insomnia. It would take me 4 to 5 hours to fall asleep. A couple of nights I did not sleep at all. It was just horrible. I did not seem to get better. I could not go out and meet up with people. I could not do any work on my online businesses for 2 months.

I was listening to a doctor on the radio who mentioned that many people had adrenal fatigue and were not aware of it. As I looked into it, I realized that I had adrenal fatigue since I had all the symptoms associated with it. Once I knew that I had the condition, I was able to figure out what to take to get better, and I started improving. It was gradual, but slowly I started getting stronger, and within a couple of months, I was close to full strength.

I started feeling better and was able to start going outside. I was able to finally see my girlfriend after 2 months. I started gradually sleeping a little bit better, and nowadays I sleep fine.

Of course while being sick and trying to recover those months, I lost business, and it took a while to start getting back the business I lost. However, my health was far more important. If you don't have your health, it really does not matter how much money you are making.

I was very grateful to my girlfriend. We had been dating only for a couple of months when I got sick. I tried going to visit her where she tutored kids one day, but I was sick and had to head back home. We lived in different boroughs of New York City. I lived in the Bronx, and she lived in Queens. We kept in touch via email during that time I was sick. I could not even get the strength to speak on the phone because of my illness.

I am so grateful that she stood by me, even though we were not together a long time. I know not everyone would have stayed with me considering we were not together that long. We did bond very well during the two months we dated before I got sick. Her emails lifted me up, and after a couple of months when I started getting better, we started seeing each other again. Since I was not at full strength, I could not stay out very long (a few hours) with her initially. In time I got stronger and stronger.

They say you should look for a pearl in a disaster. For me the disaster was my getting sick. The pearl was knowing that she was there for me, no matter what I went through or what happened to me.

Problems and Difficulties Will Occur In Your Life

One mistake people make that I used to make was spending too much time in personal development and not taking enough action. Don't get me wrong. Personal development is extremely important. I spent at least a half hour reading and also watching videos on personal development each day. The problem is if you don't take action on what you learn, then you are wasting time and your talents. You need to implement what you learn to experience success. You need to implement the knowledge you gained within 72 hours, otherwise, it will be wasted, as you are likely to forget much of it.

Another important factor for success is to keep in shape. Richard Branson said the first thing that a person should do in order to become a billionaire is to keep fit and exercise. That is because by doing so, it gives you extra energy.

One more thing to realize about being an entrepreneur is that it is a marathon, not a sprint. You will have ups and downs like a roller coaster. If one tries to go into it thinking they will get rich quickly, they are in for a big disappointment. You have to be in it for the long haul.

I was honored when I was selected to be a co-author and have a chapter in Mark Hoverson's "Million Dollar Day" book. Mark is an 8 figure earner, and I knew when the book came out, a lot of eyeballs would get in on the book.

When you are an author, you get instant credibility. You are seen as an authority. People respect you and look up to you. Once you are an author of a book, people see you as an expert because you wrote about a subject.

The vast majority of people want to write a book, but never get around to do it. Most people don't do it because of fear. They fear that people won't like their book or will laugh at them. The truth is that most people will respect the fact that you wrote a book, because you did it, while most of them wish they had written a book but didn't.
If you have always wanted to write a book, go ahead and do it. Write it and share your story. There are people who will want to read your story and be inspired by it. The vast majority of people in the United States

want to write a book, but never get around to doing it.

Since the Million Dollar Day book came out and I was listed as a co-author, a lot of people have reached out to me. I am now forever known as an author. When you tell people that you are an author, they look at you differently. You are immediately seen as an authority in your field.

There is a saying that you can't be an "author"ity without being an author. There is a lot of truth to that.

When you struggle and go through difficulties and periods of doubt in your business, realize that you are not alone. Most successful people struggled and went through a number of failures. They learned from their failures, made adjustments, and never gave up. The thing is after you hit success, you realize that it was all worth it. It's like when you search to meet Mr. or Mrs. Right for years, and feel despondent it will never happen. Once you meet the right person, you will feel the journey was worth it.

As a Catholic Christian, I realize that we will struggle and suffer and that is part of our journey. It's often not fun going through it, but you see meaning in it. In fact, those that have never really suffered or struggled often are kind of shallow and superficial and can't understand other people. I know from my own experience when my dad passed away over 10 years ago, it was devastating for me and it hurt so much. It also taught me to be more sympathetic toward other people when they suffer. I also understood people better when they lost someone they love because it happened to me. It also made me a less selfish person.

A lot of successful people often struggled through numerous failures and know how difficult it can be to succeed. That is why they often want to help people out who are starting off. They know your struggle and understand it, and often want to help you succeed.

BE PRESENT AND FOCUS ON PEOPLE

When talking with someone, it's very

important to be present with them. Have you ever spoken to someone, and you could tell that they were not fully listening to you, but were distracted and thinking about something else? Most people can tell if you are not really paying attention to them.

Successful people are excellent at being totally present with the person they are talking to, listening with their full attention, and not letting anything distract them.

Disraeli beat Gladstone for Prime Minister in the United Kingdom because he made people feel they were the smartest person in the world. Bill Clinton had a way of speaking to people that he made you feel that you were the only person in the world when he spoke to you.

People want to see that you are truly interested in them and that you care about them.

Dale Carnegie in his classic book, "How To Win Friends and Influence People," states that "You can make more friends in two months by interested in other people than in two years of trying to get people interested in you."

Carnegie is absolutely right. Have you ever spent an hour or two with someone, and they did most of the talking, and you did most of the listening? When you two were done speaking, the other person gushed about how much they enjoyed meeting with you and talking with you, and what a great conversationalist you were. Yet you did very little speaking. You just let the person talk about the person they were most interested in, which is themselves.

On the other hand, when you just talk about yourself and don't ask the other person about themselves, they start getting bored and lose interest in what you have to say. That's why dates who talk about themselves and how about great they are, are avoided like the plague. People want to date people who are interested in them and in what they have to say.

That's one reason people love dogs. Dogs are always interested in you and are always happy to see you. Dogs give an unconditional love that often many people can't give you. Dogs make you feel important. When someone makes you feel important, you can't help but like them more.

Habits

Habits are one thing that separates successful people from unsuccessful people. Successful people have successful habits, while unsuccessful people don't have successful habits. You don't need to add more habits to be successful. You just need to replace your unsuccessful habits with successful ones. Once you do that, you will start seeing great results.

They say it normally takes about 21 days or three weeks for a habit to sink in. That is why military groups often have boot camps lasting 3 to 4 weeks because they know it will take that much time for a new habit to sink in with the new recruits.

When you think about it, we are all creatures of habit. Over 90% of the things we do is because of habits that have become ingrained in our subconscious minds. Think about how you start out the day every morning. Don't you usually do the same things getting ready in the morning? You put your pants on the same leg first every day. You shower and then maybe eat some breakfast and drink a cup of coffee on your way to work. You take the same route to work, whether it's by car or by train. Has it ever happened that when you had to drive somewhere else first before going to work in the morning, you still started off on the same car route, until you realized you needed to go a different way? Why is that? It's because you have ingrained in yourself the habit of driving to the same place via the same route each morning.

Take Responsibility For Yourself

People often don't take responsibility for themselves. When something bad happens to them, they tend to blame other people or circumstances for it. They never realize the part they played in what happens to them.

This goes back to the Garden of Eden after Adam and Eve fell. Adam blamed Eve for sinning and Eve blamed the serpent, and people have been trying to shift the blame to others ever since for their own faults and sins.

One problem with not taking responsibility is that it weakens you. When you say "I can't do this," it tells your mind that you are not capable of doing it. When you say "I won't do it," it is more empowering because you are saying that you choose not to do something. Even more empowering is to say "I can do it" or "I will do it."

When you take responsibility for your actions, it empowers you. You realize that whether you succeed or not is up to you, and you are much more likely to take the massive action required to make yourself become successful.

Successful people always take responsibility for everything that happens to them. They don't blame their parents, their exes, their teachers, their bosses, the economy, the weather, etc. They know that they are ultimately responsible for whether succeed or fail.

If you are late for work, don't blame the traffic or the subway. You are late because you did not give yourself enough time to get to work. If you left 20 minutes earlier, you would definitely have made it on time.

Many people have learned to have others take care of them. There is a story of a woman who was bedridden and was looked after by her mother. She said that she could not do anything and had to have her mom do everything for her.

One day that lady's mom died. So what happened? She got up and started doing things for herself because her mom was no longer there to take care of things for her. While her mom was alive, she avoided responsibility and played a weak victim because her mom did everything, and she liked it. Once the mother was gone, no one else was left to take care of things, so she got up from her bed and did it.

When I was younger, I used to blame other people and circumstances for any bad things that happened to me. It felt easier to not take any responsibility and blame something or someone else. The problem was that I had developed an external locus of control. I did not feel that I could change what happened to me.

All successful people will tell you when they started taking responsibility for their actions, things started changing for them. It was no different for me. When I started taking responsibility for everything, I felt empowered and I took more action. Things started seeming less overwhelming for me. I started procrastinating less and got more done. I started looking at myself to take care of things, instead of waiting for other people, or for situations to change.

People make money in good economic times and in bad economic times. So you can't just say it's always the economy that determines your fate. You can do something about your future even in a bad economy. Many people start their own businesses during recessionary times when there are not many jobs out there, and a good number of them become successful at it and make millions.

If you don't succeed at something, take responsibility. No good comes out of blaming someone else. You will only annoy them or upset them when you blame them.

When you blame other people or outside circumstances, you give up power. When you take responsibility, you gain power and get a lot more done and are more productive, as well as become more successful.

You can choose to either make excuses or make results. The choice is ultimately up to you. Making excuses will accomplish nothing and will disempower you. When you choose to make results, it will empower you.

It's very important that you are proactive instead of reactive.

The questions you ask yourself are very important. Very often people focus on asking themselves the wrong questions that are negative, and they wind up focusing on the negative. They will ask themselves questions like these:

1. Why does my life suck?
2. Why can't I meet Mr. or Mrs. Right?
3. Why are all men/women jerks?
4. Why can't I make any money?
5. Why can't I get anyone to buy my products?
6. Why can't I get anyone to join my business?

The problem with these questions is that they are disempowering, and have you focus on the things you don't have. It is said that whatever the mind focuses on expands. If you keep your questions focused on what you don't have, your mind will keep steering you in that direction, and you will continue to not have any of those things you desire.

A better strategy is to change the questions you ask yourself. Focus on asking yourself empowering questions. Let's change the questions we just asked a little and notice the difference:

1. How can I make my life better?
2. How can I go about meeting Mr. or Mrs. Right?
3. How can I meet a nice man or nice woman?
4. How can I make more money?
5. How can I get people to buy my products?
6. How can I get people to join my business?

Notice that these types of questions are positive and more empowering.

Take Massive Action

Grant Cardone, in his book, The 10X Rule, talks about taking massive action. He talks about taking 10 times as much action as you think you should. Cardone talks about how people often underestimate how much time and effort it takes to accomplish something. He recommends taking massive action to accomplish your goals and dreams.

You need to put in 10 times the amount of effort most people put in to achieve success. You also will need to condition your mind for success, because if your mind is not right, you won't take the necessary action to become successful.

What often happens is that when you 10X your efforts, you will encounter more obstacles. You just need to work through and around them.

Cardone also says you need to be everywhere, all over social media and everywhere else. If people don't know about you, then you don't have a business. Everyone knows about Coca-Cola and Starbucks because they are omnipresent. Cardone tells us that we have to do the same.

<u>Comfort Zone</u>

Try this exercise. Fold your hands. Notice which thumb is on top. It will be either the right one or the left one. Now switch thumbs and put the other thumb on top with your hands folded. How does that feel? Feels kind of weird, doesn't it? That is what happens when you try something new. It feels weird and uncomfortable. However, if you leave hands folded the new way, after a few minutes, you will start getting used to it and you won't feel as uncomfortable. The same thing happens when you try something new. At first, it feels uncomfortable, but after a while, you get used to it and you start feeling more comfortable with it.

Without a doubt, one of the biggest enemies of success is the comfort zone. People may not like their situation, but they are comfortable in it. They at least know what to expect each day. That is why many people stay at a job they don't like for years, or date someone they are not happy with for years. They are not happy but they are comfortable. They fear the unknown, so they would much rather stay where they are because there is no unknown. Remember we are creatures of habit, including bad habits.

Many people are comfortable with what they are doing, and know what to expect when they go to their job each day. I have known a number of people who complain about their job all the time but never leave that job. They stay there until they get let go from the job. Not surprisingly nothing changes. Some people will stay in an unhappy relationship with their boyfriend or girlfriend because they are comfortable and fear the unknown. They fear to be without someone and prefer the comfort of a mediocre relationship. The sad thing is that if they moved on, they might wind up meeting Mr. or Mrs. Right.

That is not a healthy way to live. Staying in a miserable job will stress you out, make you unhappy, and do terrible things to your health and immune system. Similar things can happen with a bad relationship.

Sometimes you have to take a chance on the unknown. If you leave the job you hate, you may wind up at a job you absolutely love. If you leave the person you are unhappy with, you may find someone who truly makes you happy. However, you won't find that great job or great love if you stay where you are.

Yes, there are risks involved, but there are always risks in life. There's a saying that it is better to do the uncomfortable now and be comfortable later in life than to do the comfortable stuff now and be uncomfortable for the rest of your life.

The question is "Are you willing to do what is uncomfortable now so that you will be comfortable later?" I gave up and sacrificed a lot to make myself better and more successful. I gave up watching a lot of tv shows I liked. I love listening to music, but I cut down on the amount of music I listened to and replaced it with powerful, positive, motivational trainings from successful people.

Your beliefs are what you believe to be true. No matter what the world says or what your friends say, if you don't believe something is possible for you, then it won't be possible because your subconscious will stop you from succeeding.

The comfort zone is one of your biggest enemies. Never forget that. A lot of people are unhappy with what they are doing, but they fear change and the unknown. Most people are creatures of habit, and it's often very difficult to change habits.

A number of things happen when you are in your comfort zone. You won't grow as a person because you are content to be in the position you are in. Some people say if you are not growing as a person, then you are dying. What tends to happen with people in their comfort zone is that things will either remain as they are or they will eventually get harder, because situations changed and they did nothing to improve themselves.

When you are in your comfort zone, you start feeling more bored and discontented since you did not do anything to make any progress. This will often lead to a negative mindset, which means more unhappiness.

You will also miss out on opportunities that could present themselves to you if you remain in your comfort zone. You won't be as successful and you won't enjoy life as much. You wait for things to happen instead of going out there to make things happen. What often happens is that you get left behind because you never took action and never took any risks.

Frederick B. Wilcox said, "Progress always involves risks. You can't steal second base and keep your foot on first base."

Have you ever watched a sports game where one team, instead of playing to win, is playing not to lose? They don't take chances. Usually, the teams that take no chances often lose. Sometimes you'll see a football team leading in a close game in the 4th quarter play what is called a "prevent defense". They give up a lot of short 10 to 15 yard passes instead of one long 50 yard pass. What often happens is that the team playing the prevent defense often loses the game. The prevent defense only prevented a win. The teams that play a more aggressive defense in a close game usually win more often than the teams that employ the prevent defense.

You have to take chances for things to change for you. I remember at my last company when I was in the corporate world, there was a drawing at our Christmas party. We had about 35 people in the company, and only 2 of them would win tickets to go anywhere in the world. We all submitted our business cards. Some, because of certain activities they did for the company, got to submit 2 or 3 business cards. I almost did not submit my card, but then I said: "What the heck." Lo and behold, I was one of the two people who won the drawing. I wound up deciding to go to Hong Kong and had an amazing time. I also flew business class, which was awesome. If I did not submit my card, I would not have gone on that trip.

I also think back to my first mastermind trip several years ago in April 2014 in San Diego. I was a little scared of going on that trip because I knew no one there and I was pretty new to online marketing and to the company whose event it was. But I got out of my comfort zone and went on that trip, and made so many connections there that totally changed my life. I learned a lot of things there and had so many great memories there. I also met many other people through the people I met at that event.

Never be afraid to take chances. If you try something and it does not work, at least you can say you gave it a shot. However, if you don't try something, years later you may have big regrets over not trying. I had some regrets about things I did not do when I was younger. I resolved not to have those regrets later on. Jim Rohn used to say that the pain of discipline weighs ounces, while the pain of regret weighs tons.

I want to encourage you to go for those dreams. If you pursue your dreams and don't give up, no one can stop you. The only one who can stop you is yourself.

You also have to develop yourself and invest in yourself. If you don't invest in yourself, you won't get better. You can't expect people to invest in you if you won't invest in yourself.

You also have to do things that other people won't do, so you can separate yourself from the crowd. If you do what everyone else does, you will get the results everyone else does.

I was honored when one of my mentors, Jermaine Steele, asked me to speak at his event in Las Vegas in April 2016. Again it got me out of my comfort zone. It also did wonders for my confidence and enhanced my credibility. I started making changes, and have done numerous talks in public since, and have hosted my own events.

I also did a 90-day video challenge a couple of years ago. It was scary because I had never done videos. My first videos were horrible. The great thing is that as time went on and I become more confident in myself, my videos started getting better.

I also went through a 90-day blogging challenge in one of my former companies. I was not much of a blogger before doing this challenge, but the challenge got me to be more consistent.

What you have to realize that champions do the work of a champion long before they become a champion. Very often people only see you having success, but don't see all the effort you put into it and all the struggles you endured and obstacles you overcame. Most successful people are not overnight successes. They really worked their butts off and did not give up. They were consistent and made adjustments along the way.

Many Olympic athletes started practicing when they were 6 or 7 years old and practiced 4 to 6 hours every day. Many sports athletes started when they were kids and worked at it for many years. The best violin and piano players often started when they were very young.

If you try to do online marketing, you should not expect to succeed immediately. Success does not happen in a day but is done daily. Consistency is one of the major reasons people don't succeed. They say it can take up to 10,000 hours to master a subject. If that is true, don't be surprised if you haven't mastered something in a couple of weeks. It takes time and effort.

If you work your business and do the right things, there is no way you won't get results in the long run. It's like when you take a sharp ax and take 5 swings at a tree every day, the tree will eventually come down, regardless of how big it is. If you keep taking those 5 swings in your business every day, you will see awesome things happening.
I work at my business consistently 6 days a week. I take off Sundays for the Sabbath. I realize that working 10 hours a week was not going to get me huge results. I needed to put in my time and dedication to really get it going.

I am amazed at how so many people just want to get quick money, and if they don't make money in their first week in business, they get upset and quit. Many also expect big results without doing any work.

Since many people are looking for quick money, that is why many people are susceptible to scams that promise them big and quick money, and these scammers take their money and then disappear or the company falls apart. If something sounds too good to be true, it usually is.

You would not ask your boss for a $10,000 raise after your first week on the job, so you probably should not expect $10,000 in your first week in an online company as a newbie marketer. Sadly, some unscrupulous people take advantage of naive people and convince them they can make people money quickly. Those unfortunate people give their money to these unscrupulous people, make no money, and then give up thinking that all online companies are scams.

Focus on building your roots deep, and sooner or later, you will achieve big results. A great example of this is the bamboo tree. The bamboo tree spends 3 or 4 years underground building its roots and does not grow above ground. Then in the 4th or 5th year, the bamboo tree will grow 90 feet. Go and do the same and build your foundation deep like the bamboo tree.

When I used to work in the corporate world, I liked getting in early so I can do work without co-workers bothering me with phone calls and email requests.

I do the same thing now. I like to get started early in the morning, even though I work from home. I start with reading, praying, exercising, meditation and visualization. The other work follows later on in the day. Most successful people have early morning routines that get them ready for the day.

I spent a lot of time building myself up and building up my business. I built relationships with people over the course of a couple of years. I also try to go to as many events as possible so I can meet as many people as possible. It paid off after a couple of years. People started noticing me and started noticing that my business was taking off and that I was getting a lot of engagement on my posts. What they did not see was that I worked very hard for two years trying to build my business.

When I started doing weekly webinars, things really started taking off. You are seen as an authority when you host webinars because very few people do webinars. The tendency in most people is to do what everyone else does, because they feel it is the safe thing to do. The problem is that most people are not living the life that they desire, and most of them are not achieving great results in their lives.

It was scary because I was not used to doing webinars. Then I realized that with everything else I tried, I was not good at it when I started, but I got better as I continued it. It's like when I go back and watch the first videos I ever recorded, I was terrible in those videos. But when I started doing more of them, I started getting better at them.

When I started doing webinars more often, I began getting better at them. Again even in the early webinars, people still looked at me like an authority because I was providing them with value, and I was being an authority because I was doing something most people who work online rarely do, which was hosting a webinar.

If you want to be successful and have the life that most people don't have, then you must start doing the things that most people won't want to do. That is how you separate yourself from the rest of the pack.

I had a vision and I stuck to that vision. Visualizing is extremely important. You have to see it in your mind because you can see it in reality.

It's incredible when the success starts coming in, how much your confidence starts to soar. I remember when seeing sales come in on a consistent basis on my e-commerce stores, I started feeling more confident. I realized that this was going to happen day after day and that I did not have to worry too much about sales coming in.

I used to look at my emails a lot and see if anyone joined me in my business, or if I got any sales. It was not a productive use of my time, and it was a distraction. Looking at my emails was not going to make someone join me. I learned later to not focus on my emails and to focus instead on income producing activities.

The cool thing about success is that when you start getting some success, you start feeling better and more confident about yourself, and you start attracting more and more success. It is true that success builds upon success. The more confident you are about yourself, the more you attract people to you, and the more success you attract.

Confidence and belief in yourself are so critical to your self-esteem. If you don't feel confident, people sense that in you and don't want to work with you. It's like if you are not a confident guy, you won't attract too many women because they can sense that lack of confidence in you. Whereas if they sense you are confident, you are more likely to have women attracted to you.

Grant Cardone, the sales guru, recommends being omnipresent. It's not enough to be on one social medium, such as Facebook. Not everyone is on Facebook. You need to get yourself on as many social media as possible, whether it is Twitter, Instagram, Pinterest, Google Plus, Snapchat, etc. The more often people see yourself, the more likely they will reach out to you and want to work with you.

No matter how great you are or how great your product is, if people don't know who you are, no the safe thing to do. The problem is that most people are not living the life that they desire, and most of them are not achieving great results in their lives.

It was scary because I was not used to doing webinars. Then I realized that with everything else I tried, I was not good at it when I started, but I got better as I continued it. It's like when I go back and watch the first videos I ever recorded, I was terrible in those videos. But when I started doing more of them, I started getting better at them.

When I started doing webinars more often, I began getting better at them. Again even in the early webinars, people still looked at me like an authority because I was providing them with value, and I was being an authority because I was doing something most people who work online rarely do, which was host a webinar.

If you want to be successful and have the life that most people don't have, then you must start doing the things that most people won't want to do. That is how you separate yourself from the rest of the pack.

I had a vision and I stuck to that vision. Visualizing is extremely important. You have to see it in your mind because you can see it in reality.

It's incredible when the success starts coming in, how much your confidence starts to soar. I remember when seeing sales come in on a consistent basis on my e-commerce stores, I started feeling more confident. I realized that this was going to happen day after day, and that I did not have to worry too much about sales coming in.

I used to look at my emails a lot and see if anyone joined me in my business, or if I got any sales. It was not a productive use of my time, and it was a distraction. My looking at my emails was not going to make someone join me. I learned later to not focus on my emails, and to focus instead on income producing activities.

The cool thing about success is that when you start getting some success, you start feeling better and more confident about yourself, and you start attracting more and more success. It is true that success builds upon success. The more confident you are about yourself, the more you attract people to you, and the more success you attract.

Confidence and belief in yourself is so critical to yourself. If you don't feel confident, people sense that in you and don't want to work with you. It's like if you are not a confident guy, you won't attract too many women because they can sense that lack of confidence in you. Whereas if they sense you are confident, you are more likely to have women attracted to you.

Grant Cardone, the sales guru, recommends being omnipresent. It's not enough to be on one social medium, such as Facebook. Not everyone is on Facebook. You need to get yourself on as many social media as possible, whether it is Twitter,

Instagram, Pinterest, Google Plus, Snapchat, etc. The more often people see yourself, the more likely they will reach out to you and want to work with you.

No matter how great you are or how great your product is, if people don't know who you are, not one is going to buy it. A McDonald's in the middle of the desert with no people nearby is not going to make money.

You have to brand yourself and get yourself out there. Don't worry if people get sick of seeing you. If they know you, they are more likely to do business with you.

Avatar (Your Perfect Buyer)

It is important to market your business or product to the right person. Very often people try marketing to the whole world, and they up wind marketing to no one. You need to know who to market your product or opportunity to.

If you are selling high ticket items, such as a 10K coaching program, you don't want to market to people who want to pay $50 for a business opportunity. If you own a steakhouse, you don't want to market it to vegetarians for obvious reasons. You want to market to people who will be interested in your product.

I remember listening to the radio years ago to an all sports radio station where I live. This company was advertising women's pantyhose on the radio station. I remember thinking, "They are not going to get many pantyhose sales from this station as over 90% of the listeners on the all-sports station are male, and are not going to buy it." That is a case of a company not knowing it's avatar.

Before you market, you have to figure out who your ideal client is. Once you know your ideal client, then you can figure out how to market to them.

When you are trying to sell something to someone, you have to figure out what problems they are trying to have solved. They say that when a person is going to buy a drill, they are not buying the drill. They are buying the hole that the drill can give them. What is the problem that the person wants solving? They don't care about the program or the process as much as about how can it solve their problem.

Celebrate Little Successes

One mistake that many marketers make, and one I used to make as well, is to not celebrate the little successes. Many shoot for the big goal to feel successful, such as making $500,000 or $1,000,000 in a year.

The problem is that it's very difficult to make that money starting off in a year. So if you think that you are only successful if you make $1,000,000 in a year and you only wind up making $50,000 that first year, you are going to feel like a failure.

If you start celebrating the little successes, you will start feeling more successful, and that will seep into your subconscious. Success will build upon success, and eventually, you will start achieving bigger wins and successes.

In a football game when the starting quarterback gets injured, the coach knows that the backup quarterback is not as good as the starter. The coach knows that he should not have the backup quarterback try to throw 40 or 50 yard passes because he does not have the confidence the starting quarterback have. The coach instead has the backup quarterback start throwing short passes that are easy to convert, such as those of 5 or 6 yards. After the backup has made a few successful short passes, the coach then has him try throwing passes that are a little bit longer.

The same thing applies in your businesses. Instead of worrying that you need to make $25,000 in your first month or that you need to get at least 10,000 leads, focus first on making a sale or two. If you get a sale, celebrate it. Then when you get two sales, celebrate it. When you make a few more sales, celebrate it. If you made $50, celebrate it. Then when you make $100, celebrate it. Soon it will be $500 and then $1,000. If you get a couple of leads in a day, celebrate it. Then when you get 5 more leads celebrate it. When you get 10 leads, celebrate it. As you keep celebrating each success, you will start seeing yourself as a success.

You will soon see that your little successes turn into bigger and bigger successes. As you keep doing that, the successes will continue to increase.

My Struggles and Obstacles

I definitely had my share of struggles. At times it frustrated me that I was working hard and developing a lot of knowledge, yet people would often sign up with someone else. Still, I knew that I did not want to go back to the corporate world. I hated having limited freedom and having to be at work at a certain time and then not being able to leave before a certain time. I also hated the fact that I was told what to do, and my freedom to do what I liked was limited. I also hated getting emails on the weekends or on vacation from work about tasks or problems that needed to be taken care of. I did not want to see that when I was away from work. I wanted to enjoy my weekends and not worry about work. I could not go back to that kind of lifestyle. I needed to make this work from home stuff work.

Granted, I work harder now than I did in the corporate world. Still, I feel much freer because I enjoy what I do much more. And I love interacting with the people much more doing what I do now than when I did before as an employee. Don't get me wrong. I met some great people and made some wonderful friendships while I worked in the corporate world. It's just that there were some people in the corporate world I was forced to interact with, who I would have preferred not to interact with. There were also sometimes people in management I had to deal with and had to be super nice and kiss up to because they could get me fired if they did not like me. At times I felt like I was not being myself, and not being true to myself.

One of the things I love about working for myself is that I get to be myself and don't have to answer to anyone. No one who does not like me can fire me and mess up my future. My future is in my hands.

Whether I succeed or not is totally up to me. No one else decides it for me.

We all desire to be successful without going through any obstacles. The truth is there is no way that you can avoid obstacles. While they are not fun to deal with sometimes, obstacles make you stronger.

Napoleon Hill, in his classic book, Think and Grow Rich, wrote: "Every adversity, every failure, every heartache carries with it the seed of an equal or greater benefit." He was definitely right about that.

While I don't look forward to the obstacles I have dealt with, I have come to appreciate them. They have helped make me stronger and made me realize I can overcome just about anything.

One thing I learned from recovering from my sickness in 2015 was to give up coffee. One of the causes of adrenal fatigue is overuse of stimulants. I was a big coffee drinker for many years. I haven't had a cup of coffee in 2 years.

one is going to buy it. A McDonald's in the middle of the desert with no people nearby is not going to make money.

You have to brand yourself and get yourself out there. Don't worry if people get sick of seeing you. If they know you, they are more likely to do business with you.

Celebrate Little Successes

One mistake that many marketers make, and one I used to make as well, is to not celebrate the little successes. Many shoot for the big goal to feel successful, such as making $500,000 or $1,000,000 in a year.

The problem is that it's very difficult to make that money starting off in a year. So if you think that you are only successful if you make $1,000,000 in a year and you only wind up making $50,000 that first year, you are going to feel like a failure.

If you start celebrating the little successes, you will start feeling more successful, and that will seep into your subconscious. Success will build upon success, and eventually, you will start achieving bigger wins and successes.

In a football game when the starting quarterback gets injured, the coach knows that the backup quarterback is not as good as the starter. The coach knows that he should not have the backup quarterback try to throw 40 or 50 yard passes because he does not have the confidence the starting quarterback have. The coach instead has the backup quarterback start throwing short passes that are easy to convert, such as those of 5 or 6 yards. After the backup has made a few successful short passes, the coach then has him try throwing passes that are a little bit longer.

The same thing applies to your businesses. Instead of worrying that you need to make $25,000 in your first month or that you need to get at least 10,000 leads, focus first on making a sale or two. If you get a sale, celebrate it. Then when you get two sales, celebrate it. When you make a few more sales, celebrate it. If you made $50, celebrate it. Then when you make $100, celebrate it. Soon it will be $500 and then $1,000. If you get a couple of leads in a day, celebrate it. Then when you get 5 more leads celebrate it. When you get 10 leads, celebrate it. As you keep celebrating each success, you will start seeing yourself as a success.

You will soon see that your little successes turn into bigger and bigger successes. As you keep doing that, the successes will continue to increase.

My Struggles and Obstacles

I definitely had my share of struggles. At times it frustrated me that I was working hard and developing a lot of knowledge, yet people would often sign up with someone else. Still, I knew that I did not want to go back to the corporate world. I hated having limited freedom and having to be at work at a certain time and then not being able to leave before a certain time. I also hated the fact that I was told what to do, and my freedom to do what I liked was limited. I also hated getting emails on the weekends or on vacation from work about tasks or problems that needed to be taken care of. I did not want to see that when I was away from work. I wanted to enjoy my weekends and not worry about work. I could not go back to that kind of lifestyle. I needed to make this work from home stuff work.

Granted, I work harder now than I did in the corporate world. Still, I feel much freer because I enjoy what I do much more. And I love interacting with the people much more doing what I do now than when I did before as an employee. Don't get me wrong. I met some great people and made some wonderful friendships while I worked in the corporate world. It's just that there were some people in the corporate world I was forced to interact with, who I would have preferred not to interact with. There were also sometimes people in management I had to deal with and had to be super nice to and kiss up to, because they could get me fired if they did not like me. At times I felt like I was not being myself, and not being true to myself.

One of the things I love about working for myself is that I get to be myself and don't have to answer to anyone. No one who does not like me can fire me and mess up my future. My future is in my hands. Whether I succeed or not is totally up to me. No one else decides it for me.

We all desire to be successful without going through any obstacles. The truth is there is no way that you can avoid obstacles. While they are not fun to deal with sometimes, obstacles make you stronger.

Napoleon Hill, in his classic book, Think and Grow Rich, wrote: "Every adversity, every failure, every heartache carries with it the seed of an equal or greater benefit." He was definitely right about that.

While I don't look forward to the obstacles I have dealt with, I have come to appreciate them. They have helped make me stronger and made me realize I can overcome just about anything.

One thing I learned from recovering from my sickness in 2015 was to give up coffee. One of the causes of adrenal fatigue is overuse of stimulants. I was a big coffee drinker for many years. I haven't had a cup of coffee in 2 years.

The interesting thing about coffee is that it gives you a big rush like a regular drug, but then you crash a couple of hours later. Thus, you need more coffee and the cycle repeats itself.
Nowadays, I start off drinking a pint of water when I wake up. I drink water throughout the day, and I have steady energy. I never crash during the day.

It is important to be healthy and have lots of energy to succeed online. I am more productive now that I have more energy, and I exercise regularly throughout the week. My favorite exercise is walking. We were created to move around, and most Americans don't walk enough because they drive everywhere. Exercising and working out will also help you sleep better.

You have to realize that obstacles will always come your way. There is no way to avoid them. There are some you just can't plan for. Instead of hoping that obstacles will never appear, I've learned how to deal with them.

You may be successful with a multi-level marketing company and things are going well, and all of a sudden, something happens and the government shuts down your company. It's out of your control, and you can't do anything about it. You did not do anything wrong, but the company got shut down. Thus, you have to move on and do something else.

If you have developed yourself, you can take your talents elsewhere, or you can even start your own company.

<u>Friendships</u>

One of the things I love about working online is all the friendships I have made with people all over the world, many of whom I have met in person. If I had stayed working at a regular 9 to 5 job, there is no way I would have ever met these people.

Relationships are a huge part of this business. Just building that one relationship with a certain person or persons can open up many doors to you. I can tell you the relationships I have made have been key to helping me succeed.

There is a saying that your network is your net worth.

Unfortunately, many marketers try to spam their links to people all over social media. It just does not work. People have to know, like and trust you first. If a strange man comes up to a woman and asks her to marry him, she is going to reject him because she does not know him. She has to get to know him first. I will not join any person in business who I have not gotten to know first.

Entrepreneurial Game

Being an entrepreneur is not easy, but it's fun and definitely worth it. People think they can join a company online and make big bucks immediately. They also think they will get paid weekly or bi-weekly like they do at a regular job. However, entrepreneurs get paid irregularly, especially starting off. It may take weeks and even months before you get paid. That frustrates some people starting off, and many quit as a result. They don't realize that if they work at their business for months, they can eventually start getting big payoffs. Patience in this industry is definitely a virtue.

Some people go in with the mindset of "I'll try it for 30 days and if it doesn't work, I will quit." First, they are using a limited 30-day vision, which will likely fail. You need to use a long-term vision. Second, they are using the phrase "I will try", which usually leads to failure. They should say "I will make it work" or something similar. No one became a millionaire saying "I will give it a try." You have to say you will make it work.

<u>Your Mindset</u>

A lot of people underestimate the importance of mindset. I've known smart people who think they're stupid and pretty girls who think they're ugly. Even if everyone thinks you're good, smart, or pretty, if you don't believe it, it doesn't matter. It's what you believe about yourself that matters.

There are lots of talented people who don't succeed because they don't believe in themselves and in their ability to succeed. I used to be like that. I always wanted to have a lot more money, but never really believed I could do it.

When I got involved in internet marketing, everyone started talking about mindset. All of the successful people I saw were talking about mindset. There were lots of videos about the importance of mindset. I figured having a positive mindset helped a little. But is it that crucial? It most certainly is. I realized that one of the reasons I was not succeeding as much I wanted to was because of my mindset. There was a part of me that believed I could do it. There was also a part of me that didn't believe I could be successful. There were conflicting emotions. I realized that the conflicting emotions were holding me back from becoming more successful.

That is why I realized I had to change some things with my mindset. I started limiting my time with negative people because they were dragging me down with their negativity. I started interacting a lot more with positive people.

A lot of the people I know who I enjoy interacting with don't live near me. Still, there are many other ways for us to chat such as the phone, Skype, Facebook, Google Hangout, etc. This is how I interact with many positive and successful people, and it's made a huge difference for me.

You can't get rid of the negativity in your mind. Once it's there, it's there. However, I've learned that you can dilute the negativity with lots of positive messages. It's like diluting a solution of alcohol with water. The more water you add to it, the weaker the alcohol solution is. So positive and uplifting thoughts are what will make the solution of negative thoughts weaker by dilution.

One thing I like to do is say affirmations in front of my mirror. I like saying out loud, "I like myself," "I am the greatest marketer," and "I am comfortable with abundance and prosperity." It feels weird the first couple of times you do it, but as you keep doing it, you'll feel comfortable doing it and you'll enjoy doing it because you will be convincing the person you need to convince the most, which is yourself.

It is important to start your day off on a positive note and end it on a positive note. When I wake up, I listen to positive, motivational stuff from guys like Jim Rohn, Tony Robbins, Les Brown, Jack Canfield and Zig Ziglar. It's good for my subconscious mind and gets my day off to a good start. I never turn on the news first thing in the morning because it's all negative stuff: murder, stabbings, robbery, terrorist attacks, this candidate attacking another candidate, etc.

I also make sure to listen to positive stuff or read good stuff before going to bed, because it will seep into my subconscious mind while I sleep.

I also find exercising in the morning, praying, visualization, and some meditation is also helpful. Having an attitude of gratitude in the morning is also helpful. I also program in my iPhone three uplifting and positive messages that go off at 9 am 1 pm and 7 pm on my phone.

Visualization is powerful. Your mind cannot tell the difference between real and imagined events. I visualized meeting Jack Canfield. Sure enough, Jack Canfield came to give a talk near where I lived, and I got a chance to meet him, take pictures with him, and have him sign a book for me.

What happens is if you visualize something you don't have, there is a tension in your subconscious mind, and it goes to work on getting the thing you are visualizing that you don't have.

Visualization is very popular with sports stars. Basketball players visualize scoring the game-winning shot. Football players visualize scoring the game-winning touchdown or throwing the game-winning pass. Baseball players visualize hitting the game-winning home run in the world series or striking out the batter to win the world series.

You will hear many athletes say that after accomplishing a great goal, they had visualized it happening hundreds of times in their mind before it happened.

Many successful people also visualize things like the exact type of car they wanted or the exact kind of house they wanted, and years later they got the exact car or the exact house they had visualized.

Jack Canfield recommends what is called the hour of power. That includes 20 minutes of meditation, followed by 20 minutes of visualization, and ending with 20 minutes of reading.

If you are busy working a job and are driving to work, you can listen to positive, motivational stuff while driving to and from work. If you take the train to work, you can also listen to positive, motivational stuff on the train. You can always find time to listen to motivational stuff that can help you.

We live in a negative world. Growing up we heard the word "No" 8 times as often as we heard the word "Yes." No wonder most of us are negative. We've trained our minds to hear the word "No" for everything. That is one reason why people don't believe they can succeed. Too many people have told them no, and they don't believe in themselves.

The thing to remember is that negative mindsets are learned. No one is born with a negative mindset. When we are born, we are uninhibited. We do whatever we want. We cry when we want to get fed by our parents. We don't care how much we cry for things. We will continue to cry if we don't get them.

As we grow up, we learn and are told we can't do certain things. We keep hearing "Don't do this!" or "Don't do that!" After a while, you learn that you can't do certain things, and you start doubting your ability to do these things. That often affects you as an adult, and you often don't even realize it.

You start doubting your ability to do things because of what you were taught as a child.

Do you know how to train fleas? You put them in a jar. Fleas initially start jumping up and keep hitting the top of the jar. They will continue to do so and will keep hitting the top of the jar. After a while, they will stop hitting the top of the jar and will jump up a little less high so they don't hit the jar. You can then open the jar and they still won't jump any higher because they have been conditioned to do so.

Human beings are the same way. When we are born, we have no limitations on what we want to do. As we grow up, because of what we learn from parents, school, institutions, and organizations, we are conditioned to limit our beliefs in what we can do just like the fleas in the jars.

The good thing is that since behaviors are learned, they can also be unlearned. We are not doomed to forever live our lives the same way. Millions of people have been unable to unlearn the devastating behaviors that have held them back from having a happy and successful life.

A lot of people don't realize that you don't see opportunities with your eyes. You actually see opportunities with your mind. If your mind is not right, opportunities will pass you by.

You need to get rid of the energy drainers from your life. That is get rid of people who are negative and have given up on life and want to bring down everyone around them.

We all know the saying that birds of a feather flock together. If you surround yourself with negative people who like to complain and not want to do anything to make their situation better, then you are likely to become more like those complainers.

They say you are like the 5 closest people you hang out with the most. If you want to become more successful, you have to surround yourself with more successful people. I know when I started surrounding myself with more successful people, things started changing for me.

Some might say "Well I've been friends with this person since childhood. I can't get rid of him as a friend." You don't have to get rid of a person as a friend, but you can limit your time with them, especially if they are negative and holding you back.

All this shows that you have the power to change your life. You have to be proactive and change your actions. No one says it is easy, but it is possible.

I have noticed that when I am around negative people, I feel drained and less powerful. When I am around positive and successful people, I feel happier, more energetic, and more powerful.

One danger of being negative and complaining all the time is that you become what T. Harv Eker calls a "crap magnet." The more you are negative and complain about how much your life stinks, the more you will attract people who are negative and complain. When one person starts talking about how much their life stinks, someone else in the group is going to jump in and say, "Well, if you think that you got it bad, wait till you hear what happened to me!"

Do you really want to surround yourself with those kinds of people?

The thing is you tend to attract what you focus on. When you focus on negative things, you tend to attract negative things. One reason is that our brain's reticular activating system filters out anything that is not important to you, and only allows what is important to you. That is because you are bombarded with information all day long, and your conscious mind can't handle everything. So it needs a filter, which is where the reticular activating system (also known as R.A.S.) comes in and filters out unimportant stuff.

The reticular activating system is the reason why when you are at an airport and you hear all kinds of names called out by the public speaking system, your mind ignores it because it is unimportant. However, if your name is mentioned, you automatically hear it because it is important to you. If you decide you want to buy a red car, all of a sudden you start noticing red cars everywhere because it's important to you.

If you think you will never succeed, your R.A.S. will not notice when great opportunities are presented to you. It is also why people who think they won't meet a nice man or a nice woman rarely do so. Their mind is focused on meeting someone who treats them like crap, and when a nice person comes by, they either don't notice them or unconsciously reject them because they don't think they are good enough for them.

This is why you need to focus on the things you want and desire, not on what you don't want. If you want to be successful, start thinking of yourself as successful. Focus on thinking of successful images and reading and listening to successful people.

Until you have the mindset, you won't do the technical. Mindset always comes first. Believe you can do it. Stop using the words "I can't" and start using the words "I can."

Years ago everyone said that it was impossible to run the 4-minute mile. Many tried and failed.

Roger Bannister visualized himself breaking the 4-minute mile and practiced doing it. Eventually, he was able to break the 4-minute mile and ran it in 3:59.4 seconds. What was deemed impossible was now possible.

John Landy broke Bannister's record 6 weeks later. Numerous other people have run the 4-minute mile since, while before it was deemed impossible. It was only impossible because people thought it was impossible with their minds.

People talk about going on a food diet, which is awesome. What many people also need to do is go on a mental diet. You would not feed your body garbage for obvious reasons. Yet many people allow all kinds of garbage into their minds. We have heard the saying "Garbage in, garbage out." If you let garbage come into your mind, garbage will come out.

We have to be careful what we say to ourselves and what we think about all day. If you carefully watch what you say to yourself, you'll be amazed at all the garbage and negative things you are saying to yourself throughout the day.

You must pay attention to your self-talk, what you say to yourself throughout the day. Robert Kiyosaki says "It's not what you say out of your mouth that determines your life, it's what you whisper to yourself that has the most power!"

We probably talk to ourselves about 50,000 thoughts a day, although most of the time we don't pay attention to what we say to ourselves. The truth is most of the stuff we say to ourselves is negative, and it has a damaging effect on our mindset and belief in ourselves, and it interferes with our chances of becoming successful.

Subconscious Beliefs

Many of your subconscious beliefs you are not aware of. Those subconscious beliefs may be what is holding you back. The reason is these beliefs go back to when you were small. Before the age of 6, you have no judgments or filters. The more messages are embedded into your brain before 6, the more they become a part of your beliefs. So if you keep hearing from your parents and your schoolmates negative things, you will absorb those messages.

Maybe you heard one of these phrases from your parents;

1. Money is the root of all evil
2. Money does not grow on trees
3. You have to have money to make money.
4. Rich people are immoral.
5. Rich people take money from others.

If your parents fought about money while you were a child, you may think that money causes pain and is a bad thing and not worth having. You will make sure you don't have any, and even if you get some, you'll find a way to spend it.

If you want to have money and want to be a good person, there is a conflict. If you want to be a good person, then you can't have money because your subconscious mind says that rich people are immoral and take from others. You will subconsciously work to not have money because of what you learned from parents and because you want to be a good person.

When there is a conflict between logic and feelings in your mind, the feelings almost always win out in the end.

Having a bad mindset will sabotage your success just like a flat tire will sabotage your car from being able to drive at a normal speed.

The important thing is that you need to be aware of these things. Once you become aware of the fact you are sabotaging your success, then you can work on changing things so that instead of sabotaging your success, you will work on becoming successful.

Dealing with Rejection

A lot of people are afraid to ask for a sale or to ask a person to join their business because they fear rejection. Rejection is scary to most people.

One reason many people fear rejection is that they fear that they will lose something. That is not true at all. You are actually not worse off at all and have not lost anything. At worst you are at the same position you were when you began when someone rejects you.

Say I have no one to have dinner with it. If I ask a girl to have dinner with me and she says yes, then I have someone to have dinner with. If she says no, I had no one to have dinner with when I started, and I still have no one to eat dinner with. I am in the same position as when I started, and have not lost anything.

Now say you start off the day with no sales. If you ask someone to buy your product and they say yes, you have made a sale. If they say no, you have no sales for the day, which is where you were when you started the day. You are in the same position and have not lost anything.

Now you realize that when someone says no to your opportunity, you are at worst in the same position as you started. You have not lost anything. Once you realize that, you won't fear rejection as much, especially since you have everything to gain and absolutely nothing to lose.

Regrets

One of the worst things is having lots of regrets. I know when I was younger, there were some girls I wanted to ask out but didn't because I was not sure if they would say yes. Later on, I regretted it because I realized I should have taken the chance, and the worst that could have happened was that they said no. Very likely some of them would have said yes, and I would have had a few more dates and possibly a few more relationships. Later on, I resolved not to let that happen anymore. When I was interested in someone, I would ask her out. If she said no, at least I knew for certain, and would not have any regrets about not having asked her out.

When you are near the end of your life, you don't want to look back and say that you wished you had gone into business for yourself, or tried a different career, or asked this person to go out with you or marry you. At least if you tried and it did not work out, you can say to yourself that you tried.

Mentors and Investments

You can't succeed without a mentor. You will not find a successful person who does not have a mentor who has helped guide them.

Invest in yourself. If you don't invest in yourself, nothing will happen. I went to college and even though it cost a lot, I saw it as a worthy investment, as do most people who went to college. You have to do the same when you have an online business.

Many people see investing in a company or in a mentor as a cost instead of an investment. They don't see the value they get from their company trainings.

There are also people called "FreePreneurs" who just only want to get all their info for free and not pay for anything. This shows a lack mentality.

You could Google everything you need for your online business for free, but it could take you years and decades to find that info. It's a much more efficient use of your time to get a mentor to teach you and to invest in that person. Or you can invest in a company with great training. Time is more valuable than money. You can always get and make more money, but you can't get more time. Once that time passes by, it never comes back.

Trying to figure everything on your own is not a wise or productive use of your time. It is much better to pay someone to teach you, and you can succeed in a much shorter period of time.

Time is a precious asset. You can always make more money if you lose money, but you can never get more time once time passes by.

It has also always amazed me that online marketing seems to be the only industry where people think they can succeed without a mentor. A mentor will save you lots of time, money, and heartache. All great sports athletes have coaches, and all successful people have mentors.

Foreign mountain climbers have what are called sherpas. Sherpas are people who have climbed the mountain before, and who are able to guide the mountain climbers and make the journey up the mountain easier. It's much easier than climbing the big mountain yourself.

Sherpas are known as mentors in the entrepreneurial world.

Lebron James, Stephen Curry, Roger Federer and Serena Williams and other star athletes all have coaches to guide them. If the best players in the world realize the need for a mentor or coach, then realize you definitely need one to succeed.

When you try to go into online marketing, you don't know much. There is a big learning curve. If you try to learn on your own, you will make mistakes.

I know when I got started, I made plenty of mistakes. I would email strangers I did not know my company link, and needless to say, not many joined me. A few of them sent me nasty emails and blocked me. Looking back, I don't blame them for some of their reactions

My mentors helped me avoid the stupid mistakes I made when I started out in online marketing. They made me realize that spamming my links to strangers was a waste of time and that I would never build a big business that way. They showed me that building relationships and giving people tons of value would be far more effective. They taught me many other things as well.

My mentors also showed me the proper way to interact on social media. When you get yourself a mentor, that mentor will help you limit the number of mistakes you will make and will speed up how quickly you achieve success.

Obstacles

In life and in business you will always deal with obstacles. We all want to avoid them, but they are unavoidable. Your account may get shut down, or you're restricted from posting on some form of social media. You just never know when an obstacle will appear to test you.

One mistake some people do is to put all their eggs in one basket. That is dangerous because if something happens to that one stream of income, you are in a lot of trouble. You deserve better than that.

The interesting thing is that if you didn't have obstacles and struggles, you would not appreciate the things you have. There is a tendency in many to take things for granted and not appreciate the things that are just given to them.

I remember watching the movie "The Karate Kid." The kid is hoping to learn karate, but instead, he's cleaning by waxing. His teacher is telling him "Wax on" and "Wax off." The kid is furious because he doesn't think he's learning any karate. He is impatient, but he does not realize that this is part of the process and takes time. Eventually, he does become good at karate.

People act the same way when starting an online business. They want to make big money immediately, but they have to do the little things and develop themselves first. They get frustrated they haven't learned much, haven't progressed much, and haven't made much in the beginning. The thing is if they continue to be consistent, they will see the results, just like The Karate Kid did.

Henry Ford once said, "When everything seems to be going against you, remember that the airplane takes off against the wind, not with it."

There is a story of a man who watched a butterfly struggling to get out of its cocoon. It made a little progress by making a small hole, but the hole was not large enough to get its body through it.

It struggled for a long time and appeared to be exhausted and stood still.

The man felt sorry for the butterfly and decided to open the cocoon hole with a pair of scissors, which allowed the butterfly to get out free.

There was a problem. The body of the butterfly was small and wrinkled, and the butterfly's wings were all crumpled up.

The man looked to see if the butterfly would open its wings and fly away. However, nothing happened and the butterfly spent the rest of its life dragging its shrunken body around since it was not able to fly.

The man meant well by helping. However, he did not understand that the purpose of the tight cocoon and the efforts of the butterfly to get out of the cocoon was so the butterfly could train and strengthen its wings through the adversity of getting out of a cocoon. Nature set it up this way so that the butterfly could work its way out of the cocoon strong enough to fly.

What we should realize is that using some extra effort is what we need to overcome adversity and obstacles. If you don't make that effort or if it is done for you, you won't be able to handle the next obstacle or battle in your life.

That is one reason why some parents do their children an incredible disservice by spoiling them and giving them everything. Those kids often wind up with a sense of entitlement and don't know how to handle adversity and rejection, because they have never had to exert effort to deal with obstacles and never had people say no to them. Those spoiled children usually don't succeed in life.

Go to Events

The first mastermind event that I ever went to was in April 2014 in San Diego. It turned out to be an awesome event. Not only did I learn a lot there, but I made a lot of new friends.

From that one event, I got to meet many other people through the friends I made at that event. I think back and wonder where would I be if I had not gone to that event.

One of the most important things for me was meeting successful marketers like Jack Canfield, Ray Higdon, Vince Reed, John Lee Dumas and many others. I spent thousands of dollars going to these events to meet these guys. It was definitely worth it. Not only did I learn a lot from these guys, but I also met a lot of great people and made many wonderful connections because of them.

If you are in a company and they have an event, you should always go to the event. There are several reasons for it. One is that your belief will grow from being around people who believe in their dreams and will support you in your dreams. They will reinforce your beliefs if you have some struggles. There is so much negativity out there and lots of negative people who will try to stomp on your dreams. That is why it is critical to follow people who are of the same mindset and will support you.

You may learn some things that can change your business and your life. You also may meet some people such as the leaders in the company, and those relationships will help you so much in your career. If no one knows about you and your business, your business will fail. The more people you meet and the more relationships you develop, the more success you will achieve.

Every 6, 7, and 8 figure earner goes to their company events because they see the value of going to the event. Those who don't go to their company events usually don't have that much success.

At the first event I ever hosted, several of the participants implemented some of the things they learned at the event, and they started achieving big results in their businesses within days of the event! It totally changed their business and their lives. Amazing things happen when you come to events.

<u>Take Action</u>

Many people wait for the perfect time when there are no problems and conditions are perfect before they take action. The problem is that there will never be a perfect time where everything is perfect and there are no problems. When certain problems disappear, other new ones will appear.

The best time to start taking action is now. You can always make adjustments and improvements along the way. That is what successful people do. You will also learn more as you start taking action. There is a big difference between theory and practice. You can read all the books about becoming successful. Until you actually start taking action, nothing will happen to you and nothing will change. When you start taking action, you will learn as you go along, and you realize that the practice is far more important than the theory.

When a rocket is sent to the moon, it is off-course most of the time. However, the rocket keeps making adjustments along the way, and it eventually has a perfect landing on the moon.

A similar thing happens with a plane that goes from New York City to Los Angeles. The plane will be off-course most of the time, but it will keep making adjustments along the way until it lands perfectly at Los Angeles Airport.

Your plans will change along the way. You will make adjustments and improvements along the way. I know I am constantly making adjustments and improvements in my businesses. The great thing is that I started, and because I started, I am able to get to the finish line. If I never started, I would never have gotten anywhere.

There is a saying that imperfect action will always beat perfect inaction.

When you learn something new, you should implement as soon as possible, otherwise, you will forget it. In fact, if you read books all the time, learn all the success quotes and principles and never take action on any of the stuff, then you are wasting your time. It has to implemented within 2 to 3 days after you learn it, otherwise, you will forget it.

Jim Rohn used to say that you should never trust your memory. If you learn something useful, write it down. No matter how good you think your memory is, you will often forget something if you don't write it down. Once you forget, it is gone forever. When you write it down, you have saved it and can go back to it.

Have you ever woken in the middle of the night and thought of something great, but then went to back to sleep, figuring you would remember it in the morning? What happened later? Most of the time you forgot the brilliant idea you came up with. It would have been better to write down the idea, and then go back to sleep. This way you could look at it in the morning when you woke up.

I used to go to bible study for several years before I was asked to take up a leadership role. I led many sessions in the bible study over the next five years, and my knowledge of the faith increased exponentially. Why was that? Because I agreed to lead, and took action and started reading more commentaries and preparing for my lessons. If I did not step up and take action as a leader, my faith would not have been as strong and I would not have been as knowledgeable about my faith.

You don't need to know everything to get started. You just need to get started and you will learn as you go along. I did not know everything when I became a bible study leader. I learned along the way when I became a bible study leader.

Jack Canfield in his book, "The Success Principles," talks about how at a seminar he hosted he held up a $100 bill and asked who wanted a $100 bill he was holding in his hand. Naturally, most of the people raised their hand. Some even shouted that they wanted it or to give it to them.

Jack calmly stood there calmly holding the $100 bill until they "got it". Eventually, a woman jumped out of her seat, rushed to the front of the room, and took the bill from Jack's hand, and went back to sit down.

What did the woman do that no one else in the room did? She got out of her seat and took action. She did what she had to do to get the money.

When asked why they did not go for the $100 bill, people responded with statements such as they did not think it was real, or they did not want to look foolish going up for it and not getting it, or they did not want to look needy for the money.

It turns out that many of these same excuses are what prevent us from taking action.

You must take action if you want to succeed in life, and the sooner you do it, the better.

Many people wait for the perfect time to arise before they take action. What often happens is that the perfect time never arrives because there is always some new problem or obstacle that arises. The perfect time to start is always now.

Zig Ziglar used to remind us that you don't have to be great to get started, but that if you want to be great, you have to get started. Nothing changes until you get going. You will also learn more as you start doing.

Many people want to master the theory first before taking action, but until you take action, you won't accomplish anything. You can continue learning the theory while taking action, and you will learn a lot more that way. There is nothing quite as good as experience.

What Do You Desire?

Too many people focus on what they don't want instead of focusing on what they want. When you ask what they want, they will talk about what they don't want. They will say, "I don't want a boss," or "I don't want to go to work." They don't talk about what they want.

Try to get them to see what they want. They want to travel the world, or play golf or go to the beach more often. They may want to go see all their kids' games or piano recitals. They may want more time freedom. They may want to buy their parents a house or retire their parents and spouse. Those are the things that will inspire people to work and take action.

Too many people let the opinions of other people stop them from pursuing their dreams. Don't let others steal your dreams. Focus on your dreams, and let them focus on their own dreams or lack of dreams.

Never Give up Three Feet From the Gold

I have seen many people give up. The sad thing is that many of these people if they had not given up, would've succeeded. There were many times where I felt like quitting, especially when I got sick. However, I realized that if I gave up, nothing would change for me. I would still have the same problems I had before. I realized that for things to change for me, I would have to change. I never forgot the story from Napoleon Hill's "Think and Grow Rich" where R.U. Darby and his uncle gave up digging for gold just 3 feet from the gold. They sold the machinery to someone else, and that guy winds up making a lot of money when an engineer told him that the previous guys quit 3 feet from the gold. R.U. Darby at least learned his lesson and later became one of the most successful insurance salesmen in the country. He never gave up after an initial no from a person. He persevered and got many of the people who said no initially, to say yes to buying insurance from him.

I did not want that kind of regret. I figured if I persevered and did not quit, things would work out for me.

Lots of people failed a lot but persevered, and as a result, became very successful. Thomas Edison failed almost 10,000 times before he succeeded in inventing the lightbulb, and that's why we don't use candles in our homes anymore. Abraham Lincoln lost the vast majority of races he entered until he was elected President in 1860. George Washington lost all but two battles during the Revolutionary War. The final one he won was the one where Cornwallis surrendered to him in Yorktown in 1783. Cornwallis surrendered his sword to George Washington and said "Sir, I salute you. Not only are you a great leader of men, but an indomitable Christian gentleman who wouldn't give up." What we learn from these people is that Failure plus Perseverance equals Success.

Napoleon Hill discusses in his book, "Think and Grow Rich," how when the money starts coming, it then starts coming easily. Then you wonder where was this money all this time.

When a rocket tries to leave the earth, it spends most of its fuel in trying to leave the earth and its orbit. Later on, when the rocket has left earth, it flows freely and very easily, almost as if it is doing no work.

You have to do the same. You have to do the work and build the foundation. It may take a while, but once you do, the money starts coming in, people start offering to do partnerships with you. Lots of great things happen because of all the time and effort you put in. You will build up huge momentum because of your efforts.

Some people say that you get underpaid while developing yourself and working hard on your business and that later on you get overpaid because of what you did in the past.

The truth is most successful people have put in lots of time, energy and effort into succeeding. It rarely happened overnight for them.

Olympic athletes will practice 4 to 8 hours a day, 6 days a week, for many years before they make it to the Olympics for a chance to win a medal.

You just have to take action and put in the work.

There is an old joke about a guy who was praying for 20 years to win the lottery. One day he gets fed up and asks "I've been praying for 20 years to win the lottery, and week after week goes by, and I don't win. Why????" He then hears a voice that says "You must buy a ticket first."

Credibility & Authority

A big problem for many people is having credibility and authority. If you have amazing results from your business, then you definitely will have credibility with people. But what if you don't have those results. How can you build credibility and authority without results?

There are several things you can do. If you are on social media you can start posting a lot of value, that is things that are useful to people in their internet marketing business. Many online marketers keep posting their links, again and again, hoping that people will join them. Posting value helps separate you from many marketers who are simply spammers.

Another thing to do is do lots of videos. Many people are afraid of doing videos and have trouble getting out of their comfort zone. It can be scary doing that. The truth is that when you start making videos, you're going to stink. It's not surprising. You stink at anything that you start doing. However, if you keep working at it, you will keep getting better and better.

If you start hosting webinars, your credibility with skyrocket. Very, very few people host webinars, so if you start hosting webinars, your credibility will grow. You are doing what very few people do. All of the big marketers do webinars, and it's a big money earner for them.

Host your own events. Very few people host their own events. When you host an event, you are automatically seen as an authority. Think about all the events hosted by people. When you hear those people speak at the event, you automatically assume that they are authorities and know what they are talking about.

When I hosted my first event, my credibility skyrocketed. Lots of people started reaching out to me to become friends on social media, and a number of people reached out to me for coaching. They saw me as an authority because I hosted my own event.

Write your own book. Authors have a great deal of credibility. When you tell someone that you are an author, people automatically assume that you are an authority in your field and very knowledgeable. The truth is most people want to write a book, but rarely get the courage to do so. So when they meet someone who has actually written a book, they will see them as an authority.

If someone wrote a book on diets, you would assume they are an expert on diets. If they wrote a book fishing, you'll assume that they are an authority on fishing.

So write a book on a subject you are good at and publish it. You will forever be an author, and people will see you as an authority. The vast majority of people in poll after poll want to write a book, but for a variety of reasons never write a book.

Once you do all these things to differentiate yourself from everyone else, you will start seeing awesome results that most of the other people are not getting because they are not taking the action you are taking.

Get Started Now and Don't Procrastinate

The best time to get started is now. I used to procrastinate a lot. I then did Mark Hoverson's Million Dollar Day, and after doing, it I learned to eliminate procrastination.

The thing is when you procrastinate, you have a lot of unfinished tasks, and those unfinished tasks create a big psychological burden on you, and they often wind up stopping you and paralyzing you from doing other things.

Successful people do not procrastinate and take action immediately. They don't let unfinished tasks multiply.

One thing I used to do when I worked in the corporate world was that I would let a lot of things pile up on me. This piling up of unfinished tasks would later become a psychological burden me, and it would prevent me from finishing tasks. I found that procrastination would paralyze me sometimes when I would look at the unfinished tasks that lay before me. That is what happens to most people who procrastinate.

There is no perfect time to start. If you are always waiting for the perfect time and the perfect conditions to happen, you'll be waiting forever. The perfect time and perfect conditions don't exist. You think if one or two problems disappear, then the time will be right to get started. The truth is that problems will keep appearing. You will have problems and obstacles happening and occurring throughout your life.

You just need to get started and take action, and you will overcome any problems or obstacles that happen.

There is a joke where a person says he is going to stop procrastinating, starting tomorrow.

One of the biggest problems people have is with procrastination. Procrastination is one of the biggest killers of success. I use to procrastinate a lot. I never realized just how procrastination prevented me from achieving success until I did the Million Dollar Day.

The purpose of the Million Dollar Day is based on if a millionaire offered you a million dollars to do a bunch of tasks in a day, would you be able to do it?

Basically, one of the major reasons we don't accomplish all of our goals and desires is because of procrastination. We either say to ourselves "I can take care of this later" or we fear to do a task, so we put it off as much as we can. The problem is if we put it off till later, that task does not go away.

One of the reasons companies put expiration dates on coupons is because they know that if they don't put expiration dates on coupons, people will procrastinate using the coupons. When the person realizes he only has a week to use the coupon otherwise he'll lose it, he will use the coupon.

Ever notice that you work hard on your project right before it's due? Or you cram for a test the night before? Or you do your packing the night before you leave for a trip? You also work hard the day before you leave the office to go on vacation. Football teams play with high energy when they are trailing late in the game, and go into the two-minute offense.

Why don't these people and teams play and work with high energy all the time? If that football team played consistently, they would play much better.

One of my mentors told me how one of his rich friends showed him his suitcase which was filled with clothes. My mentor asked him where he was going, and his rich friend said, "Nowhere, but if I decide to go on a trip, I'll be ready to go at once." This is a person who is prepared and does not procrastinate.

One thing that I learned from the Million Dollar Day is that when you procrastinate and don't take care of tasks, it becomes a psychological burden that paralyzes you and prevents you from doing your tasks. Once you take care of those tasks, then it frees up your mind, and you will be able to become more productive and proficient.

When I used to work in the corporate world, my desk always used to be messy. I always wanted to keep certain papers in case I need to look at them. I noticed that all the big executives had spotless desks.

No doubt some people who looked at my desk thought I was not in control of my life. People who have a lot of clutter at their desks or at their home usually have a lot of clutter in their mind, and they don't accomplish as much in their lives.

When I started doing the Million Dollar Day, I cleaned up the clutter on my desk and in my rooms. It was amazing how much better I felt. When I used to look at my room and see clothes on my chair or on my drawer instead of in my drawer, I would feel paralyzed and not know what to do.

I am now much productive and efficient in what I do because I procrastinate a lot less, and as a result, I have become a lot more successful.

It is easier to get things done and be more productive when it's easier to find what you need. Ever have that problem that it took you an hour to find a report or print out because your work area or home was a mess? That was an hour of wasted time that you could've used for doing something productive. Those hours add up to a lot of wasted and unproductive time over the years.

If you are not achieving the success you desire, ask yourself if you are procrastinating. Take a look at the things you have left undone for a long time. Take care of those unfinished tasks, and notice how much better you will feel.

A little bit of procrastination can cost you a lot of time and money. Mark Hoverson in one his trainings describes how because he waited 5 minutes to call a vendor, it cost him 5 days. At 4:55 he decided to wait 5 minutes to call. When he called at 5:00 pm, the person he needed to talk had just left for the day. That person was not at work at the next day. Nothing could be done over the weekend. On the following Monday Mark was busy with a bunch of different things. He was not able to speak to the person he needed to until Tuesday. 5 minutes cost him 5 days. Those kinds of things happen to us all the time when we procrastinate.

Brian Tracy, in his book "Eat That Frog", says that most people in the morning work on the smallest and easiest tasks each day, thinking it will make the day go much better and much easier. Tracy argues that they are doing it the wrong way and that they should do exactly the opposite. When you handle the simpler tasks first, you still dread doing the bigger tasks later, and you will continue to procrastinate on it. Your productivity suffers as a result.

He recommends tackling the bigger tasks, which he calls eating that frog, first. When you eat that big frog first, that is handle the big task first, all the other smaller tasks will seem much easier to handle. You will procrastinate less and get more done because you don't have any big daunting tasks ahead. You ate the big frog, and now you can eat the smaller frogs and handle the smaller tasks much more easily.

One other thing to keep in mind with big tasks is that you don't have to look at it as one huge to task to handle. If you look at it that way, you will very likely feel overwhelmed. Remember the answer to "How do you eat an elephant?" is "One bite at a time."

You can do the same thing with very big tasks. You can break it down into smaller tasks (sometimes also called "chunking down"). When you break down a big task into several smaller tasks, it seems much easier to handle and finish. You will also feel a lot less overwhelmed and will complete it much more easily.

Protect Your Reputation

The most important thing you have is your reputation. Developing a good name and reputation takes a long time to build, but just a short time to destroy.

You need to take care of every one of your customers for several reasons.

First of all, a satisfied customer will keep coming back to buy from you. It is easier to sell to a previously satisfied customer than it is to obtain a new customer. It actually costs 5 to 6 times as much to get a new customer as it does to keep a current customer. Since that is the case, what makes more sense? To keep the current customer, or go try and get some new ones? Obviously, it makes more sense to keep the current customers.

That does not mean you don't try to get new customers. Of course, you should. What I am saying is that you always try to keep your current customers happy and let them know that they're special. When their birthday comes, wish them a happy birthday. Let them know of specials and offers you have coming up.

Second, satisfied customers are your best advertisement because they add to your credibility. Word of mouth is your best advertisement. When a person tells a friend they loved your product, that friend will trust them and will be more open to buying your product.

When you have a dissatisfied customer who does not like your product or service, they are very likely to go public with it and tell all their friends. Think about it, when someone writes a restaurant review online, who is more likely to write a review, someone who enjoyed their meal or someone who either hated the service? It is usually the person who is unhappy with the service. Negativity seems to multiply much more quickly than positivity.

If you give a bad product or bad service or scam someone, it will spread quickly, especially in this digital age. I have seen people who destroyed their reputation by trying to make a quick buck by scamming people. Word got out quickly that this person is a scam artist, and now no one will work with them. It will take that person a very long time to restore their reputation. It would have been better had that person been more honest and ethical and not scammed people. Maybe they would not have made as much money up front, but long term they would have made a lot more because they would have developed an excellent reputation where people would not be afraid to buy from that person.

Always think long-term and look at the big picture. When you do, you will be much more successful. Too many people and frankly too many companies look at the short-term picture and their short-term numbers, and because they don't have a long-term vision, wind up losing big time in the end.

There are no shortcuts to success. Many of those successful businesspeople, stars, and celebrities often struggled for years and never gave up, which is why they eventually hit it big.

I work very hard in trying to be honest with everyone I interact with. People always talk about you, whether you realize it or not. It's better for them to say good things about you. It is a small world, especially in this digital age. You don't want a couple of people to say that you are unethical, rude or a liar.

WHITE SHIRTS PASSING THE BASKETBALL

I teach people something I learned from Jack Canfield. It's based on a study by Daniel Simons and Christopher Chabris. I show them a video of a group of people in white shirts and a group of people in black shirts. The audience is asked to count the number of times the people in the white shirts pass the basketball to each other. After the video ends, I ask how many times did the white shirts pass the ball to each other? We get all kinds of answers, such as 13, 14, 15, 16, and 17. The correct answer is 15, but that's not the main point.

I then ask the people who noticed the gorilla walking through the group. Very few people notice the gorilla. Then I play the video again, and it's obvious that the gorilla is walking through the group of white shirts and black shirts, and even stops in the middle to beat his chest. This time everyone notices the gorilla because they are looking for him.

Why was that the case? Because this time everyone was looking for the gorilla. Before that, no one was looking for him. They were only looking at the people in white shirts pass the basketball.

This is what happens to many people in life. They only focus on looking for certain things and don't notice anything else around them. If you don't think there are any opportunities out there and don't look for them, you will not notice them, even if they are right in front of you, just like the people did not notice the gorilla in the video.

If you look for opportunities, you are much more likely to notice them.

Commitment

One of the reasons most people don't succeed is that they are not fully committed to it. If you are not fully committed to achieving your goal, you will never achieve it.

I know when I am not fully committed to something, I often don't achieve it. When I am fully committed to something, I find that I will achieve it.

People look at what other people have and feel envious of them. What they don't realize is that these people have it because they are committed to it.

Many people say that when they start seeing results, they will start committing to their business. They have it backward. You need to commit to your business first, and then you'll start seeing results.

Napoleon Hill in his classic book, "Think and Grow Rich," talks about how the Ford V-8 motor came about.

In the early 1930's Henry Ford decided he wanted a V-8 motor built. Ford wanted the engine built with 8 cylinders on one block. The engineers designed the motor on paper but agreed that it could not be built. They said it was impossible to build.

Ford told them that he wanted it built anyway. They told Ford it was impossible, but he insisted that they build it and that he wanted it built. He told them to stay on the job, no matter how much time it took.

Six months went by and nothing happened. Then another six months went by, and no motor still. They went back to Henry Ford and told him they had no luck. They were not able to build the V-8 motor.

Ford told them "Go right ahead, I want it, and I'll have it." Sure enough, the workers were able to find a way to build the V-8 motor. Henry Ford's determination and persistence won out in the end. Their limited imaginations did not alter his belief that it could be done.

This story shows that we often limit ourselves by our limited imaginations. If we expand our imaginations, like Henry Ford was able to do, we are capable of great things.

Focus

Focus is extremely important. When I started working in internet marketing, I made the mistake many newbie marketers make of joining a new business opportunity every two or three weeks. This is a phenomenon known as shiny object syndrome or shiny ball syndrome.

There is also a tendency for many people to try to do 3 to 4 tasks at a time. Lots of people think they can do several things at once. The truth is that human beings can't multitask like computers.

The best thing to do is to perform one task at a time, and then when you finish, you move on to the next task. When you do it that way, you will see that you will be far more productive, and will accomplish a lot more.
When I used to try doing several things at once, I found I was a lot less productive. When I tried doing one task at a time, I found I was much more productive. In fact, studies show that multitasking can reduce your productivity up to 40%.

I have learned to be like the hourglass. The hourglass goes from the top to the bottom one grain of sand at a time. We need to be the same way. Work on one task at a time.

One reason multitasking does not work is you get a lot more distracted when you try doing 3 or 4 tasks at a time, and the distractions are a big reason why your productivity goes down when you multitask.

In fact, if you start and stop a task, put it down, and get back to it later on, it can slow the time you finish by as much as 500 percent. One reason is that of the distractions you encounter.

Another reason it takes a longer if you stop and start again later is that of the loss of momentum. Sometimes it takes a lot of momentum to get started on something, and then as you work on it, the amount of energy needed to work on it diminishes a lot, but you still get a lot done. Once you stop, it's almost as if you are starting all over again, as you have to put all that energy to get going again and build up all that momentum.

Successful executives under this concept very well. That is why when an executive is in an important meeting or is reviewing an important document, they tell their assistant to make sure no one bothers them. They want to focus on the task at hand with no distractions.

I shut off my phone when I want to concentrate, visualize, or meditate. I do this because it is so easy for me to be distracted. I try to not respond to emails first thing in the morning. I try to set a certain time of the day where I respond to emails because if I spend all day responding to emails, I won't get a lot of work done and will be less productive.

Too many people spend a lot of time on little things that don't grow their business and not enough time on income producing activities.

Many successful entrepreneurs shut off their social media like Facebook when they want to work on an important project because they want no distractions. They turn on the social media after they are finished.

I also have learned to focus one company at a time. When I did that, I became a better marketer. I recommend to any marketer, especially a new marketer, to work at one business opportunity. Don't add a second business opportunity until you have been successful in your first business opportunity.

The **80/20 Rule (a.k.a. the Pareto Principle)** is one of the best things I ever learned. It taught me that 80% of my productivity will come from 20% of my activities.

The Pareto Principle was discovered by an Italian economist named Pareto while working in his garden. He noticed that 80% of the peas in his garden came from 20% of the peapods.

Many businesses and entrepreneurs utilize the 80/20 Rule for success because it works. Not all activities carry the same weight. 80% of your results will come from 20% of your activities, while the other 80% of your activities will give you only 20% of your results. So you need to focus on working on the 20% of the activities that are giving you 80% of your results.

Modeling Others

One thing I've learned to do is model others. Tony Robbins said, "Long ago, I realized that success leaves clues and that people who produce outstanding results do specific things to create those results. I believed that if I precisely duplicated the actions of others,

I could reproduce the same quality of results that they had."

I came to realize that I was wasting a lot of time trying to learn and do everything by myself. You can waste many years trying to do things by yourself. What I needed to do was learn from successful people, and model what they did. It's all been done before, so why try and reinvent the wheel? Of course, I made my own little tweaks and put my personal stamp on it, but once I learned to model what successful people did, things started changing for me, and I started seeing more success.

I learned that successful people act and think differently from everyone else, and that is why their results are far greater than that of most people.

Trying to do it on your own is really difficult. I know when I started in internet marketing after leaving the corporate world, I had many struggles. One big reason was that I did not know what I was doing.

Trust, Rapport, and Relationships

Very often when dealing with others, people often have a defense shield put up because many of them, consciously or unconsciously, and are afraid of being hurt or scammed, especially if they have been burned before. The thing to realize is that their defensiveness has nothing to do with you. You are not the reason they don't immediately fully trust you. Still, you have to break down the barriers with these people and show them that they can trust you.

One big mistake people make is that they immediately try to sell a product or try to get the person to immediately join their business. The other person immediately senses that all you are interested in is to make a sale or to recruit someone. I was guilty of making this mistake too when I started.

You have to first reassure the person that you are on their side that you care for them, and that you are truly interested in them. When you do that, they are more likely to trust you. We have all heard that people don't care how much you know until they know how much you care. It really is true.

It is important to build the relationship, listen to the other person, and build rapport with the other person. Show them that you are alike in some aspect, and make them feel like you understand them. If you build rapport with them and they feel you have things in common and are alike in certain ways, they are going to like you. Guess what, we all want to work with people who we think are a lot like us.

Ask them questions about themselves and what they are looking for. When people feel heard and understood, they are more likely to like you and trust you. People work with those they like and trust. Once they feel that you truly care about them and that you are in rapport with them, the sale becomes much more likely.

Always remember in the presence of rapport, anything is possible. In the absence of rapport, the sale is highly unlikely.

Have the other person come up with what they are looking for and what problem needs to be solved. Human nature needs to be consistent, so once they tell you the need, repeat the need to them again, and they will agree with you, because of their need to be consistent.

As I mentioned earlier, listening is very important. Your ears will always be more important to your sales and marketing success than your mouth will be. People love to talk about themselves. The more you let them talk about themselves, the more they will like you and think you are a great conversationalist. If they do 80% of the talking, they will say what a great conversationalist you were. If you do 80% of the talking, they most likely won't like you all that much.

Never underestimate the importance of listening. Listening is one of the most important principles for success. Every successful entrepreneur and salesperson is an excellent listener.

There is a saying that you were born with two ears and one mouth, so you should use the ears twice as often. The problem is that many salespeople do the exact opposite and talk twice as much as they listen. Not surprisingly, they usually lose the sale.

Too many salespeople talk themselves out of a sale. They get into a good rapport with a client, and then instead of asking for the sale, they keep talking and soon the client loses interest, and the salesperson loses the sale.

Men sometimes do this with women. A guy will have a conversation with a woman, and instead of asking for a date while the conversation is going well, he'll keep talking, then the rapport is lost, and she loses interest. When he asks for the date later, he doesn't get it.

People want to see that you understand their needs and that you care about them. The best way to find out is to ask them. When I say ask, I mean ask like a friend.

Don't ask questions like an interrogating prosecutor. If you do that, you will definitely lose the sale. If you talk to the person as a friend, it's easy to come up with questions to ask because when you talk to friends, you are genuinely interested in them, and want to know what is going on with their lives. The more you do this with a prospect, the more they will like and trust you.

Until they like and trust you, they will never buy from you.

There are many people out there who have had at least one bad experience with a salesperson, so they often put up a defense shield the next time a salesperson is talking to them, even if they are interested in the product.

The thing to remember is that this is not personal. You did not do anything wrong and you had nothing to do with what happened to that person in the past. It's just because they have been burned, they are afraid of being vulnerable and being burned again. That is why it is necessary to show that you are on their side, and that you care about them and not just the sale. When you are able to do that, their defenses will come down. You need to reassure them that you are there to help them and that if they are not interested, that is ok with you.

Be focused on the other person. When people see that you care about what they say and do, they will like you more. It's one of the reasons so many people like dogs. Dogs give unconditional love and are always happy to see you.

Don't Worry About What Others Think

One thing that stops a lot of entrepreneurs from succeeding is that they worry too much about what other people think about them. I used to be like that. I worried too much about what I posted on social media and worried what my friends would think of me posting stuff that was entrepreneurial.

What I came to realize is that no one was thinking about me too much. In fact, people rarely were thinking of me, and when they were thinking of me, they were probably thinking about what I was thinking of them.

The truth is that for most people, they are concerned about themselves, not about you. They are the most important person to themselves. They are wondering about their dreams, desires, and problems, and really don't have much time to worry about your life.

Most of our worries are for no good reason. They are imagined.

The other thing is that you are living your dreams, not someone else's. Focus on building your dreams. There may be a few who criticize you anyway. So what? Are they paying your bills? If not, then you shouldn't be too worried about them. There is a saying that broke people give broke advice.

I have learned not to listen to people who never succeeded because they don't truly know what success is. I learned to model and listen to successful people, because they know what they are doing, and have succeeded in life.

If you want advice about how to keep physically fit, wouldn't you rather take advice from a fitness trainer who's in excellent shape and exercises and eats well? You would not take fitness advice from a couch potato who is 150 pounds overweight and never exercises.

Don't take advice from your single friends who have a history of terrible relationships and are bitter toward the opposite sex. Their advice will be toxic.

You would not learn from Tom Brady how to shoot a basketball, or from Eric Clapton how to play the violin.

Similarly, if you want advice about how to succeed in your own business, why would you take advice from someone who's either never succeeded in business or who have never even tried to succeed in business? You want to ask advice from someone who has succeeded in business and can give you useful advice that can help you take your business to the next level.

You also don't want to fall prey to approval addiction, where you feel you need the approval of all the people around you before you take action on your dreams. If you wind up doing that, you will always be dependent on other people's approval before doing anything. We all know that people can be very fickle sometimes, and if you wait for their approval, you will never accomplish anything.

What I have found is that when you do what you want to do, and accomplish your dreams, people will approve of you more and accept you. Stand up for your beliefs and desires, and people will respect you.

It's amazing how we fear offending people, but if we are ourselves and do what we desire, people will like us for who we are and will respect us more. When you try to be someone else, and are just kissing up to people and are overly accommodating to them, some will take you for granted and will walk all over you, and won't respect you as much.

I am not saying don't be nice. You should definitely be nice. What I am saying is be yourself and shoot for your dreams and don't worry too much about what other people think. When you live your dreams instead of someone else's dreams, you will be much happier. Many of the happiest people I know are those who are living the life they want and not the life others want them to live.

I know plenty of people who went into a field their parents wanted, and they hated it and were miserable in it. Some of them eventually left the field they were in and switched to what they truly liked, and were much happier in it. They often were more successful because they were passionate about what they were doing.

You will see some successful sports stars who will tell you that they love playing the game, and they would play it for free. That's how much they love the game. Because they love the sport they are playing and are passionate about it, they gladly do the things they need to do to be successful and work hard at being successful in the sport. You will always work harder at the stuff you are passionate about.

Many people will join an online business opportunity solely for the reason of making money, but they are not passionate about what they are selling. Thus, they don't work as hard at the opportunity. The other problem is that if you are in a business opportunity and you are not making money after a few weeks, you will most likely quit and join another company. That's because your heart is not in it.

Now if you are passionate about what you do, you will put all your energy and effort in into it, and you will be more patient if you don't make money immediately because you love what you do. Maybe you are a health enthusiast, and you join a health and wellness opportunity. You enjoy being healthy and you enjoy trying to help other people get healthy. So even if you don't make some money immediately, you will be patient until you do make some money because you love the health and wellness field.

I have to admit that I fell prey when I started online to join business opportunities solely for the money. Needless to say, since I was not passionate about the opportunities, I quit when I saw I was not making money. I learned to focus on opportunities that I truly loved and was passionate about. I enjoy all of what I do now and don't dread doing it when I get up each day. That is a great feeling.

<u>Enjoy Your Life</u>

I've seen some people become workaholics. Their job or their career become their life. In some ways, it becomes an idol for them. There are several problems with this. When you spend all of your time at your job, you don't spend time with your family, friends and loved ones. You miss out on the time you can spend with them. It will also damage your personal relationships in the long run.

Working non-stop can lead to stress over the long-haul, and do damage to your health. Stress is rampant in our society.

One of the many reasons for the Sabbath in the Jewish and Christian religions is not only to spend time with the Lord and family but also to rest. Like a computer or other machine that is used non-stop and never turned off, a person who is always working will eventually break down like the machine does, unless he gets some periodic rest.

The other problem is if your job is your life, and you get let go from your job, you are incredibly devastated because you have made it your life. What else do you have to look forward to? You gave up everything else for your career.

Workaholics are often stressed out and are not very happy.

I am not downplaying work. As I mentioned earlier, I work very hard. Work is very important as many people spend up to a third of their lives at their jobs. You should enjoy the work you do. However, work should never become your only priority and the most important thing in your life, to the exclusion of everyone else.

The most successful people also enjoy life. Successful people do work hard but work is not their entire life. Successful people don't spend 18 hours a day, 7 days a week for 40 years working. Why would you want that life, if you are always working and not having fun? At a minimum, you should be taking at least one day off to have fun, relax, and clear your mind.

Our mind gets hit with so many things that we need to clear it out. A day of relaxation and fun is very helpful. Go away on a trip or vacation with your family, or at least get away for the weekend. You will have a lot of fun, create some great memories, and come back refreshed and ready to work.

On your deathbed, you won't say "I wish I had spent an extra weekend finishing up that project at work." You are more likely to say "I wish I spent more time with my kids," or "I wish I had gone on vacation more often and seen more of the world."

Studies also show that people who go away on vacation live longer. That is another incentive to enjoy life. You will come back from your vacation relaxed and refreshed, and live longer.

OVERCOMING FEAR

One thing that stops most people from succeeding is fear.

Some people describe fear as False Evidence Appearing Real. When you think about it, most of the things we have feared happening, never came to pass.

I used to fear that if I did not do well on a particular exam in school, that my life would be ruined. Of course, that was never the case. It was something I feared that never happened.

I feared that if I asked a girl out and she said no, then I would never get over it and would be hurt forever. That never happened either. I might feel disappointed if she said no, but I eventually moved on.

Mark Twain once said, "I've had a lot of worries in my life, most of which never happened." If you think about, that is the case with most of us.

Fear served a purpose in caveman times. It alerted you to possible dangers such as animals nearby that could attack you. It would encourage us to do a fight or flight response. The thing is that we usually are not near any dangerous animals that can attack us, but the fear instinct remains with us. We fear many things that rarely happen to us, and that fear often paralyzes us and prevents us from taking action.

Don't try to avoid the fear. Face it and do the thing you fear. Taking action is a great way to overcome fear. The more often you do the thing you fear, the easier it becomes and the less often you will fear to do it.

A great book on overcoming fear is "Feel the Fear and Do It Anyway" by Susan Jeffers, who tells us that it's ok to feel the fear and face it head-on. She also advises against pretending the fear does not exist.

OUTSOURCING AND DELEGATION

One of the things successful entrepreneurs do is that they outsource and delegate much of their work to others, and focus on the things only they could do or that they like.

I remember the first event I went to hosted by one of my mentors, Nate Obryant, in Dallas. I saw the people on his team constantly working that weekend on their Macintosh laptops. It hit me immediately why Nate was able to make a million dollars that year. His team did much of the work, and he was able to focus on the big things that only he could do. He taught them everything he knew and was able to duplicate his efforts with his team. I've seen my other mentors work in a similar way. They outsource their less important tasks to other people and focus on the most important tasks and the ones they enjoy doing. When they get an assistant and outsource their tasks, they wind up working less, vacationing more, and making a lot more money.

I used to imagine that I could not outsource most of my work before. However, over the past year I have outsourced much of my work, and have focused mostly on income producing activities and the activities I enjoy doing.

It has been said that you can't make more than $250,000 without an assistant. It has also been said that if you don't have an assistant, then you are one. In the beginning, you may need to do all or most of the work yourself. However, if you want to get to the next level, you need to get at least one assistant and start outsourcing many of your tasks.

The tasks you hate doing or are not good at, you should outsource. You will never enjoy or be good at doing something you hate. For example, I don't like fulfilling orders. So I outsource that task to others.

I used to shovel my snow to save money, even though it was tiresome and time-consuming. Now I focus on the big picture. I have the kids in the neighborhood shovel my snow. I figure it's better to pay them $50 and spend that hour or two trying to close a deal that can make me $500, $1,000, or $2,000. Plus, I help the economy by paying those kids, and hopefully, they are also learning a couple of things about becoming an entrepreneur.

Think about it. How often do you see a millionaire mow his own lawn? It just doesn't happen. Millionaires would rather pay someone to mow their lawn or shovel their snow and focus on money producing activities that will make them a lot more money.

That is the secret. Focus on money producing activities and outsource the lower level activities and those activities you hate.

I remember when I worked in the corporate world, you did not see high-level executives do lower level stuff that was time-consuming. They paid other people to do that. No executive was calling to confirm a trade or a deposit in an account or was trying to reconcile an account. It was done by other people while they did higher-level activities that they were paid to do.

Naturally, they delegated many of their tasks to their team.

I know when I go to an event hosted by some very successful entrepreneur, he has many people working to get the event working well, while he focuses on hosting the event.

Michael Gerber in his book, The E-Myth, discusses how often people realize that they are good at something, say baking, technology, accounting or something else, and resent working for a boss. They don't like working for someone else. So they decide to go into business for themselves, thinking it will be a piece of cake.

They wind up wearing several different hats. They wind up trying to build their own blog, website, setting up their own membership sites, running ads, autoresponders, editing videos, etc. What these people don't realize is that they can outsource many of these activities cheaply to someone else and focus on the main tasks of their business. Since they wind up trying to do everything by themselves, they wind up becoming overwhelmed and eventually give up.

In the book "The Power of Focus" by Jack Canfield, Mark Victor Hansen and Lester Hewitt, they discuss why you should focus on the things you do the best. The things you don't do well you should give to those who do it well and like to do it. The best in any field do not focus too much time on the things they are weak at. They give that task to other people to do because it's too time-consuming and energy draining to focus on things you are weak at.

DREAM STEALERS

There are a lot of people out there who are dream stealers. They don't like seeing other people succeed.

You will find that some of your friends, who you think would be happy for when you start succeeding, actually will not support on your journey. One reason is that they are jealous of you. You are doing things with your life they only dream of doing. For whatever reason, they could not do it.

Another reason they won't support you is that you and they are on two different levels now, whereas before you were both at the same level. To be at the same level again, one of two things has to happen. First, they can try to improve themselves and work on themselves to become more successful. Or they can try to bring you down to their level by disparaging what you're doing and accusing you of stuff such as being conceited and having a swelled head. Sadly, for many people, it's easier to bring people down than it is to bring themselves up and improve themselves.

You have to be aware of these people who will steal your dreams. Remember these dreams are your dreams, not theirs. Don't let them stop you from pursuing your dreams.

I have learned not to listen much to people who haven't succeeded or who haven't even tried to be successful. They haven't achieved what I am looking for, and they don't know what is or is not possible.

Negative, dream stealing people can talk you out of pursuing your goals and dreams. What many people don't realize is that negativity is much stronger than positivity. All you need is one negative person to drag down a group of happy, positive people.

Have you ever noticed that a negative player on a sports team adversely affects the play of the entire team? That is why a team full of talented players sometimes does not play as well as they are capable of playing. They may have a player or two who is talented but very negative, and they act as a distraction and cancer to the other players.

Some teams are aware of this, which is why you sometimes see them trade a talented but negative player for a couple of players who may not be as talented but are team-oriented and positive. Often the team plays much better with the less-talented but positive players. You will also hear players say they are happy the negative attitude player was traded because he was bringing the team down.

I have learned to listen to very successful people and those who have accomplished a lot with their lives. They know that you can achieve your goals and your dreams with persistence and determination. They will support you in your ventures and won't knock you down.

It's very important who you surround yourself with. They say you are the average of the 5 people you associate with the most. So if you are surrounding yourself with negative people who are always trying to knock you down, perhaps it's time to get some new friends who are happy to see you succeed.

If you don't have those kinds of people near you in your town, you can make friends with successful people online. There are all sorts of social media and programs online such as Skype and Google Hangout that allow you to talk to people all over the world. You can talk to them every week to mastermind and support each other. I have done that with numerous friends who live in all parts of the world. Many of them I have not personally met (although I plan on doing so one day), but I feel close to them because we talk a lot on google hangouts and online internet calls.

The Compound Effect

The compound effect is something whose power many people don't comprehend. Very often we don't see results quickly, and we give up. If a man wanted to have a muscular body like Arnold Schwarzenegger, he would not expect to have big muscles after a couple of workouts. He would have to go work out at the gym consistently over the course of many months, as well as eat a proper diet and exercise. As long as he consistently does it, he will start seeing bigger muscles after a certain period.

Some of you may be familiar with the question "What would you rather have, a million dollars or a penny doubled for 30 days?"

Many people would take the million dollars. The reason they choose a million dollars is when you double a penny, you go from $.01 to $.02 to $.04 in 3 days. After 8 days you have $1.28, and after 12 days you only have $20.48. It does not seem like a lot. However, soon great things will happen because of the compound effect. On day 18 you have $1,310.72, and on day 22 you will have $20,971.52. On day 26 you will have $335,544.32. On day 31 you will have $10,737,418.24, which is 9 million more than if you took the million dollars straight up. Those who understand the power of the compound effect would have taken the penny doubled over 31 days.

If you are building a foundation, it may take a while, but after some time, the compound effect sets in, and you will one day start getting huge results.

Weldon Long and Nick Vujicic

A lot of people think that because of what has happened to them, they can't overcome their obstacles and succeed. There are two successful people who prove that statement to be totally false. They are Weldon Long and Nick Vujicic.

1) Weldon Long was a career criminal and self-described loser. Weldon discusses in his book, "The Power of Consistency," how he was in prison in 1996 when he heard that his father had died. Weldon came to the realization that he had wasted his life by his criminal acts. He decided that he wanted to change his life, be a good person, be successful and be a good father to his son.

The problem was that he had 7 years to go on his prison sentence. Weldon decided to work on himself while he was in prison. He would write a letter to his son every week so that he would keep up communication with him while locked up. Long worked on his mindset and got rid of all negativity. He got his bachelor's degree and MBA while in prison. He was a model prisoner. When he got out, however, he had trouble getting a job because as soon as they discovered that Weldon was a felon, they decided not to give him the job. Weldon was very discouraged after a while because no one seemed willing to hire a guy who was a felon.

He decided to continue and eventually found one company that was willing to hire him as an air conditioner salesman. Weldon was extremely successful and became the number one salesman for that company. He quit after a year and started his own company. Weldon Long is now a successful businessman and motivational speaker and has done over 20 million in sales.

Weldon Long's story is indeed very inspirational.

Tony Robbins said to him "Quite a story, Weldon! Congratulations on your turn around from prison to contribution."

2) Another person who proves that your circumstances don't stop you is Nick Vujicic. If there was one person who had a reason to say that the odds were stacked against him and that he had every reason to not succeed, it was Nick Vujicic. Most of us have two arms and two legs, and many still complain that life is unfair. Nick was born

with no limbs. That's right. Nick has no arms and no legs.

You can only imagine how difficult it would be growing up with no limbs. It was extremely hard for Nick and he struggled with depression and loneliness growing up. He tried understanding and living with the fact that he was very different from all the other children. He questioned whether he had a purpose.

Nick, later on, started experiencing a transformation, which he credits to his faith in God, as well as the help from family and friends. Nick is now a motivational speaker, actor, author, and musician. He is married with 4 kids. His Christian faith gives him hope and helps give him a positive outlook on life. He is truly an inspirational person.

If Nick Vujicic can overcome such incredible odds to lead a successful and fulfilling life, what is your excuse?

Final Thoughts

You need to write down your goals and review them daily, preferably once in the morning and once at night.

People who don't write down their goals, follow through on them about 4% of the time. People who write them down will follow through on them about 44% of the time.

That means you are 1,100 times more likely to follow through on your goals if you write them. That is one major reason why successful people write down their goals.

Say affirmations with emotion. If you keep repeating affirmations without emotion, nothing will change. The things we remember in our lives are the ones with strong emotions attached. It could be the day you got married, the day of your first kiss, the birth of your baby, the day you graduated college, won a championship in your school, got promoted at work, etc. We remember the things that have strong emotions, and they affect us much more strongly than the events with which little or no emotions are attached.

So if you want to change the way you feel, say your affirmations with strong emotion, whether it's something like "I deserve money," "I attract money easily," or "I am more and more successful every day," say it with emotion. Your subconscious mind will believe it more strongly.

You must do what most people won't do to get the results most people are not getting. If you do what everyone else does, then you will get the results everyone else is getting, which is not much. The difference between extraordinary and ordinary is that little "extra" you give.

People who are more successful than you are usually not that much smarter than you. They either are more consistent than you are, or they are doing an extra thing or two that you are not doing. A couple of tweaks here or there can make all the difference.

Many people love the idea of success but are not willing to do whatever it takes to become successful. Are you willing to do whatever it takes to becomes successful? The truth is for many people, the answer is no.

Do you have a strong why? Maybe your why is to retire your wife, or spend more time with your kids. Maybe you want the freedom to travel the world and go traveling without having to ask a boss for permission.

Whatever product or service you are selling, make sure you own it and use it. Many people struggle because they don't own or use the product or service they are selling. Once they actually own it, they believe in it more, and they start selling a lot more.

Believe in yourself. Many of us developed our beliefs from other people's illusions. They meant well, but they hurt us with what they taught us.

Einstein said that we should become people of value. When you become a person of value and you share your value with other people, then people will want to join you and do business with you.

Jim Rohn used to tell people not to wish that things were easier, but to wish that they were better. And that makes all the difference. When you become better, you can handle all adversity.

Your income will rarely exceed your personal development. All of the most successful people I know spend a lot of time and money on personal development because they know it's worth it for them to become wealthier.

How much time are you spending on personal development? If it's only a half hour a week, then don't be surprised if you are not getting the results you desire. You need to spend more time on it because what you have inside of you will greatly affect what happens on the outside.

Many successful people become broke, and they are then able to become millionaires again because of the fact they have developed themselves. They are able to rebound from such a horrible setback because they know what they are capable of and have done it in the past.

People who are not true entrepreneurs focus on where they are. They also focus on what they don't have, what they lack, and the reasons they can't succeed. Because of this misguided focus, it prevents them from doing the things that can change their lives.

Some of the things these people wind up not doing as a result of focusing on where they are, including not buying a course or attending an event that could change their lives, or not hiring a mentor who could take them to the next level.

These non-entrepreneurs consider themselves realists. They look at what is probable instead of what is possible. The problem is probable will never get anyone to take massive action and take the risk that will lead them to huge success.

A few non-entrepreneurs do take some action. However, they do it with a "see if it works" or "test it out" mentality. They don't go all-in in their business, and instead just dip their toes in the water. They don't burn the boats to only focus on one outcome.

People who take a "see if it works" attitude almost always fail.

If you want to be successful as an entrepreneur, you will have to desire that new life more than the praise of your friends and family, and more than you care about the criticism of other people.

You have to realize that you may be made fun of and laughed at again and again by people. You need to develop a thick skin to become an entrepreneur because people will constantly tell you that what you're doing will never work. You'll be told to be "realistic" and "pragmatic" about life. They will try to project their limited visions onto you. You will have to resist their influences. That is why it will be critical to surround yourself with a group of like-minded people who will support you in your dreams.

Entrepreneurs will keep working and trying until they succeed. Non-entrepreneurs will quit as soon as they experience some difficulty.

The most important word for entrepreneurs is "until." You have to say that no matter what happens, you will keep working "until" you see success, no matter what obstacles you encounter.

Are you willing to work until you get at least 5 leads a day? Are you willing to work until you get at least 5 signups a week? Are you willing to work until you get at least $1,000 a day in your e-commerce store? Are you willing to invest in courses and attend a certain number of events each year to achieve your breakthrough?

The sad truth is that most people are not willing to do that. They will quit at the first sign of difficulty, and then complain about why life is unfair and that they are helpless to change their circumstances.

Conclusion

I thank you for joining me on this journey. It's been an honor and pleasure to have you read my book. I would love to hear from you with your thoughts, comments, and questions.

You were born to be successful. You have everything in you to lead the successful life.

I believe in you. You have so much talent and ability to do great things with your life. The question is, "Do you believe in yourself?" The truth is if you don't believe in yourself, nothing will change for you. Various studies show that only 1 in 3 people have high self-esteem, which is one of the major reasons people don't succeed and accomplish more in life.

One of the saddest things is wasted talent. Many people waste their talent and don't use what they are given. It is sad because if most people used the talents they had, it is amazing what this world would become.

Maybe you'll find the cure for some disease, build schools that help the poor and destitute, or feed millions of poor people from your success. There are so many other things you'll be able to do if you believe in yourself, and utilize the talents that you have. Just realize that you have it in you.

Go out there, make the world a better place, and make the most of your life!

God bless!
Victor Dedaj

Email me at victordedaj@victordedaj.org, follow me on Facebook at http://facebook.victordedaj.com, on Instagram at victordedaj, and on Twitter at @victordedaj

Visit my web site: http://victordedaj.com

www.ingramcontent.com/pod-product-compliance
Lightning Source LLC
Chambersburg PA
CBHW071431180526
45170CB00001B/298